wait
ahrein
India   Macao
Hong Kong
Philippines
Malaysia   Sabah
Singapore   Sarawak   Brunei   Gilbert Is.
Seychelles   Indonesia
ar   Ellice Is.
Solomon Is.
Mauritius   New
Reunion   Hebrides   Fiji
Tonga
Australia

P O L Y N E S I A

s
Rep.
uerto Rico
Virgin Is
St Martin
itts   Antigua
evis   Guadeloupe
Dominica
rrat   Martinique
incent   St Lucia
Barbados
re   Grenada
Tobago
e l a   Trinidad

University of London
Institute of Commonwealth Studies

COMMONWEALTH PAPERS

General Editor
Prof. W. H. Morris-Jones

X
Problems of Smaller Territories

Edited by
Burton Benedict

COMMONWEALTH PAPERS

I. *The Vocabulary of Commonwealth Relations.* S. A. de Smith, 1954.
II. *Imperial Federation: a Study of New Zealand Policy and Opinion, 1880–1914.* Keith Sinclair, 1955.
III. *Richard Jebb and the Problem of Empire.* J. D. B. Miller, 1956.
IV. *The Investigation of National Income in British Tropical Dependencies.* A. R. Prest, 1957.
V. *The Inter Se Doctrine of Commonwealth Relations.* J. E. S. Fawcett, 1958.
VI. *The Commonwealth and Regional Defence.* W. C. B. Tunstall, 1959.
VII. *The Nyasaland Elections of 1961.* Lucy Mair, 1962.
VIII. *Political Parties in Uganda, 1949–62.* D. A. Low, 1962.
IX. *Population Characteristics of the Commonwealth Countries of Tropical Africa.* T. E. Smith and J. G. C. Blacker, 1963.
X. *Problems of Smaller Territories.* Edited by Burton Benedict, 1967.

Guide to Resources for Commonwealth Studies in London, Oxford and Cambridge, with bibliographical and other information. A. R. Hewitt, 1957.
Union List of Commonwealth Newspapers in London, Oxford and Cambridge. A. R. Hewitt, 1960.

Problems of Smaller Territories

Edited by
BURTON BENEDICT

UNIVERSITY OF LONDON
Published for the
Institute of Commonwealth Studies
THE ATHLONE PRESS
1967

Published by
THE ATHLONE PRESS
UNIVERSITY OF LONDON
at 2 Gower Street, London WC1
Distributed by Constable & Co Ltd
12 Orange Street, London WC2

Canada
Oxford University Press
Toronto

U.S.A.
Oxford University Press Inc
New York

Printed in Great Britain by
WESTERN PRINTING SERVICES LTD
BRISTOL

CONTENTS

Introduction   I
BURTON BENEDICT

1. Demographic Aspects of Smallness   11
T. E. SMITH

2. The Smaller Territories: Some Political Considerations   23
D. P. J. WOOD

3. Some Economic Problems of Small Countries   35
A. D. KNOX

4. Sociological Aspects of Smallness   45
BURTON BENEDICT

5. Case Study: British Honduras   56
D. A. G. WADDELL

6. The Grand Duchy of Luxembourg   68
K. C. EDWARDS

7. The Consequences of Smallness in Polynesia   81
R. G. WARD

8. The High Commission Territories with Special Reference to Swaziland   97
J. E. SPENCE

9. Tory Island   113
J. R. FOX

10. Legislative-Executive Relations in Smaller Territories   134
A. W. SINGHAM

Appendix   149
Bibliography   150

MAPS

The Smaller Territories   *endpapers*
The Pacific Islands   80
Tory Island   112

INTRODUCTION

Burton Benedict

SCATTERED over the globe are a vast number of small territories. Many are islands. Some are small enclaves carved out of a larger country or continent by a colonizing power. Others are independent nations. Since the end of the Second World War, many of the islands and enclaves have become politically independent. More are in the process of doing so. Twenty years ago an independent Trinidad or Gambia was hard to imagine. Today, both are actualities. Will they be followed by an independent St Helena or an independent Gibraltar? What sort of independence can such small territories have? How can they defend themselves? How can they survive economically? How can they administer themselves? How can they provide for their increasing populations? Can they hope to maintain, or even improve, their standards of living? What political forms can they develop? What are the social consequences of living in small territories?

In October 1962, the Institute of Commonwealth Studies of the University of London instituted a seminar to investigate these problems and to attempt to discover how far there were problems common to all small territories. The seminar ran for two years. The papers in this volume are presented substantially as they were written in 1962–64. There were two sorts of papers: general papers, discussing political, economic, sociological, and demographic aspects of smallness; and case studies examining particular territories. Most of the case studies concerned the Commonwealth, but a few non-Commonwealth territories were included, notably the minute island of Tory off the Irish coast and the successful long-established nation of Luxembourg. The seminar also heard a paper on Arab unity. These papers presented some valuable similarities and contrasts to the Commonwealth papers. Yet, even within the Commonwealth, the variety of problems presented by the territories considered was immense, ranging from the small island colonies of Polynesia to the High Commission Territories in southern Africa, from the vast underdeveloped island of New Guinea to the highly populated, prosperous colony of Hong Kong. A complete list of the papers given appears in the Appendix. For this volume, it has been necessary to make a selection but all papers have contributed greatly to the discussion and to these few introductory notes.

A persistent problem for the seminar was the definition of a small territory. Was the primary criterion to be area? This would make Hong Kong small and the Aden Protectorate large. Was it to be population? This makes Hong Kong large and the Aden Protectorate small. Was it to be population density? Clearly, one could cite densely populated countries such as India and Indonesia which it would be ludicrous to term small. Mr Smith has considered these problems in his paper on the demographic aspects of smallness. But the questions of area and population, when considering smallness, are complicated by a number of other factors. Many of the territories the seminar considered were isolated or geographically remote, and this proved to be an important dimension in considering the problems of smallness. The positions of Hong Kong, Gibraltar, or Luxembourg clearly give them advantages denied to the Falkland Islands, Polynesia, or the Seychelles. The geographical positions of small territories are important variables in considering their economic and political futures. This point occurs throughout the papers and is particularly clear in Dr Ward's study of Polynesia.

From an economic point of view, smallness takes on other dimensions, many of which are discussed by Mr Knox. The reliance on a single or a very few primary products for export is a distinguishing feature of many small territories, making them peculiarly vulnerable to fluctuations of the world market. Yet some large underdeveloped countries have similar reliances and could be said, from this point of view, to have small-scale economies. Another feature of the economies of small territories is their diminutive internal markets, forcing them to rely largely on imports. Again, this is a feature which could be found in larger underdeveloped territories. Stockpiling is apt to be prohibitively expensive in small countries. This means that fluctuation in demand is more disturbing. The problems of maintaining a wide range of machinery where there is a very small number of each type, and of training and employing experts to run and repair them, may limit or delay production in small territories. It was argued in the seminar that the only way in which smaller countries can compete is to accept a lower rate of return on the factors of production. Income per head will be lower than in a large country producing the same range of products. This, it was maintained, was the cost of being a small country, but it was found difficult to determine just how great this cost was. What is the level of smallness at which costs of producing at a sub-optimum level become important? What is the cost to these countries of lessening the degree of specialization because of imperfect competition?

Large industrial enterprises can rarely be financed locally in small territories. This means that capital must be sought from outside. This raises questions not only about the costs of such enterprises but about their control. As Dr Waddell shows for British Honduras, it is by no means easy to acquire such capital, partly because of uncertainty about the political stability of the country, partly because of costly failures in the past, and partly because of ignorance of the country's economic potential.

A heavy price of independence for small territories is the cost of administration. A considerable portion of the national income of a small country may be eaten up by administrative costs. An improvement in standards of living requires heavy investment in education. Often a painful and politically delicate decision has to be made as to whether to stress universal primary education or technical and higher education for a few. The latter course, although it may improve the economy, is apt to create an elite which monopolizes positions of power and prestige and encourages political discontent. Many small territories which export their best graduates for further education abroad have the greatest difficulty in inducing them to return to their homeland. Universal education, on the other hand, even at the primary level, often produces large numbers of semi-educated young people competing for a very few white collar jobs and also leads to political unrest. Education was the largest single item of government expenditure in Mauritius for many years. In 1963, for the first time, expenditure on public assistance exceeded that on education—an ominous sign for the future. Health services are also very costly for small territories.

Solutions to many of these problems may be sought in the combination of small countries through regional and international agreements to help their exports and pool their services. Regional agreements might increase specialization and hence productive efficiency, for example Jamaica might produce all the cement for the West Indies. This would increase the market for a product and give the larger grouping a greater bargaining power *vis-à-vis* large producers elsewhere. The best example of a solution along these lines among the cases presented in this volume is Luxembourg. Here is a small country specializing in one industry, steel, which accounts for 80 per cent of the value of its total national product. It is highly integrated economically with surrounding countries, and yet maintains a considerable degree of economic independence. Of course, it has special advantages in its geographical location, the possession of large iron deposits, and the proximity of prosperous neighbours. Yet it shows that economic integration can be combined with political separateness. Such a solution might be profitable for British Honduras, which is now economically unallied.

The pooling of services would also be a great advantage in small countries. The economic development of such territories requires a wide range of equipment and a large number of experts to maintain and repair it. Few small territories can afford to keep stocks of extra parts for all the machines they need. The delays in securing replacements often slow down, or even halt, development projects. A central stock-pile of such parts on which a number of territories could draw might alleviate this difficulty, but, of course, it is only practicable where the territories are not too far from one another, as in the West Indies. Isolated territories like the Seychelles or the Falklands could not make such arrangements. A similar point can be made for experts. It is very costly for each small territory to train its own set of experts, nor can they be kept fully employed. This means that experts have to be recruited on a contract basis, paying the world market price. A pool of experts for small territories might represent a considerable saving for each of them. Savings could also be effected by the pooling of certain administrative and technical services. The British Virgin Islands shares its police force with Antigua and Montserrat, and its judiciary services with the Windward and Leeward Islands. A similar arrangement is made for government audit services. This kind of pooling of services makes for greater impartiality. As the paper on sociological aspects of smallness shows, impartiality is difficult to achieve in small territories. The pooling of government services is apt to raise political objections. Again, it is difficult to arrange for very isolated territories.

Many small territories (e.g. British Honduras, Trinidad, Fiji, Guyana, Mauritius) are plural or multi-racial societies, composed of peoples of different ethnic origins, cultures, religions, languages, and traditions. This aggravates the problems of smallness, especially where certain occupations become the exclusive province of given ethnic groups. Competition is limited and social mobility reduced. Political tensions are increased. In Mauritius, for example, there was a reluctance on the part of some business men to make their companies public for fear that members of another ethnic group would buy into them. In Fiji, the restrictions on allowing Indians to buy land have been a constant source of trouble. In Guyana, the political alignment of Indians against those of African descent has obscured all other political issues, making the emergence of Guyana as a unified nation very difficult.

Some small territories have been able to reap certain economic advantages by making special concessions to foreigners in their laws. Liechtenstein, Bermuda, and the Bahamas have all become tax havens, the former as a place where companies can be conveniently registered, the latter two both for the registration of companies and for individuals seeking escape from heavy income tax or death duties. The Channel Islands are in a similar position. Such territories have often become free ports with low or non-existent customs and excise duties. Yet another source of revenue for such areas is gambling. The Bahamas, Monaco, and the Isle of Man are obvious examples. Tourism is another rich source of revenue for such territories, which is, of course, assisted by gambling and free port facilities. It is clear that geographical location is an important variable here. The West Indies, the Bahamas, and Bermuda enjoy the twin advantages of a sunny climate and proximity to the vast tourist markets of North America. The Isle of Man, the Channel Islands, Liechtenstein, Gibraltar, and Monaco are all within easy reach of highly populated and highly developed areas. The isolation of the islands of the Pacific and Indian Oceans has so far denied them these markets. One other legal device has been used profitably by at least two small countries, Panama and Liberia. This is the 'flag of convenience' by which foreign shipowners have been able to register their ships in these countries.

The political solution to smallness would seem to lie in integration within a larger territory, federation with neighbouring smaller territories, or some relationship of clientship with a larger territory. The United Nations recognizes three ways in which a non-self-governing territory can attain self-government: emergence as a sovereign independent state, free association with an independent state, and integration with an independent state. The latter two are only valid if freely entered into by the dependent territory, which retains the right to dissociate itself. Dr Wood discusses the problems raised by these various 'solutions'. The geographical factor is clearly an important variable. Isolated islands tend to develop an autonomy which makes it difficult for them to be integrated, or even federated, with other territories. This was one of the causes of the failure of the Federation of the West Indies. It seems that some sort of economic integration or association is easier to arrange than political integration or federation.

With the contraction of European overseas empires, some small territories have acquired strategic importance. Yet the growth of nationalism sometimes frustrates the maintenance of bases on such territories. The political difficulties in the Maldives is a recent example. In 1965, some very small island dependencies of Mauritius and the Seychelles were constituted as a separate colony, the British Indian Ocean Territory, under the Governor of the Seychelles. This has elicited cries of anguish from Mauritius, which is due to become independent in 1967. In some cases, leasing bases has been a useful source of additional income, but it is clear that only a few territories can benefit from this.

If political factors make federation difficult, they form an even greater obstacle to integration. There are plenty of examples: Gibraltar, Cyprus, Gambia, the High Commission Territories. Gibraltar is still a British colony besieged by Spanish claims. Cyprus is independent but torn by dissension between Greeks and Turks. The Gambia, too, is independent, having failed to integrate with Senegal. Two of the former High Commission Territories are independent, but all three are having difficulties in their relations with South Africa. Mr Spence deals with this problem in reference to Swaziland. Swaziland is more fortunate than Lesotho (formerly Basutoland) and Botswana (formerly Bechuanaland) in that it is relatively rich in natural resources, but, like the other two territories, it is economically very dependent on South Africa. Perhaps Swaziland can become a sub-Saharan Luxembourg, but it is hard to envisage such a future for Lesotho and Botswana. Lesotho, in particular, is economically almost totally dependent on South Africa. This raises recurring questions about the smaller territories: How far can economic and political dependence be separated? How far can an economically dependent territory maintain political independence? When does economic integration become political integration? These questions are not confined to small territories, as the recent history of relations between members of the Common Market shows. Yet, a France is in a much stronger position to effect an economic and political withdrawal than a Lesotho. We may find that the symbols of political independence, acquired with such difficulty and imbued with so much emotion, turn out to be mere trappings in the face of economic competition or external threat.

Lack of economic opportunities, increasing demand for manufactured consumer goods, the spread of education resulting in higher economic and social aspirations, increases in population, the increase of information about opportunities and excitements elsewhere, have all been factors inducing emigration from small territories to large ones. As Mr Smith points out, large-scale emigration has far greater effects demographically on small territories than on large ones. The emigrants are usually drawn from the working population in their twenties and thirties. Often, they are the most skilled and enterprising. Emigration, except in a very few cases like the Cocos Islands, has been unplanned. The results may be a marked change in the sex ratio and/or the age structure of the population, sometimes reaching a scale which threatens the viability of the economy. An extreme example is Tory Island, analysed by Dr Fox. In 1962, all the marriageable girls had emigrated to the mainland for winter jobs. The age structure of the population has undergone a radical change. In 1901, the population exhibited a more or less normal pyramid. By 1961, it had assumed an hour-glass shape, due to the absence of the middle age groups (*v.* Figure, *infra*, p. 117). Montserrat shows a similar phenomenon. Both islands live largely on remittances. Emigration has reached a stage in Pitcairn Island which will soon require the evacuation of the entire population. There will not be enough able-bodied men on the island to manhandle a boat through the dangerous rocks and reefs to land. Dr Ward shows a persistent movement in Polynesia from the small outlying islands, which are becoming depopulated, to the larger ones.

The direction of migration from small territories is towards major urban centres, not other small territories or rural areas. Dr Waddell shows that British Honduras is a country which could use many more settlers for rural development, but it has not been successful in attracting immigrants. The reason is not just the reluctance of migrants from other territories to settle on the land in British Honduras, but the high cost of settling them. British Honduras cannot afford to pay for this and most territories with excess population cannot afford it either. Mr Smith cites a similar project for settling Mauritians in North Borneo (Sabah), which came to nothing for the same reasons.

Dr Fox shows how migration has been built into the social structure of Tory. Young men and women are expected to go to the mainland to work. He stresses that it is part of the life cycle, a *rite de passage* like baptism or confirmation. A similar point could be made for the High Commission Territories where men are expected to go away to work. In Tory, both male and female migrants often marry on the mainland, returning to Tory only for holidays, and so depopulation increases. Land loses its importance, for the economy is no longer based on the land but on the earnings of migrants. Montserrat is in a similar position. As Dr Ward shows, once a small island abandons subsistence agriculture, whether because of emigration or because the land is given over to cash crops, emigration is apt to increase. People must now work for a wage to buy their subsistence and there are rarely enough such jobs for the population, even if it does not increase. The demand for consumer goods and a higher standard of living grows. If possible, people leave. If not, as in Mauritius, *per capita* income declines and great poverty may ensue.

Sociologically, an outstanding characteristic of smallness is the coincidence or overlapping of roles so that individuals are tied to each other in many ways. This makes impartiality or impersonal role-relationships very difficult to maintain. This is discussed more fully in the paper on sociological aspects of smallness, but it has serious consequences in two fields: the development of medium- and large-scale industry and administration. The efficient operation of medium- and large-scale industry depends to a considerable extent on being able to hire and fire people on the basis of their performance on the job. This is very difficult to do in a small-scale society. Too many ties of kinship, friendship or patronage bind together employer and employee, shopkeeper and customer, government official and member of the public. Who an individual is rather than how he performs becomes a major criterion in the economic and political fields. In small-scale enterprises which do not require a high degree of specialization, this may not be so disadvantageous. Small-scale cash cropping on a family basis is often successful, especially where large inputs of unpaid labour are required. On Tory, kinship ties are used for recruiting and holding together crews of fishing vessels. Commercial and trading firms are often run on a family basis. Here kinship ties bind the members of the firm together, assisting them in taking risks which a firm which held its employees only on the basis of their occupational roles might not be able to contemplate. But a large factory cannot run on this basis. Efficient technical skills must outweigh personal ties.

In the internal political structure of small-scale societies, the prevalence of multiplex role-relationships and the difficulties of maintaining impersonal standards is marked. These features are clearly brought out in Mr Singham's analysis of legislative-executive relations. The pervasiveness of government in any small territory means that very few enterprises are possible without government support, and very few avenues of upward mobility fail to involve the government. As Mr Singham indicates, party politics tend to resolve into the 'ins' and the 'outs'. Political issues become structured in terms of personal encounters. The politicians who are in power reward their supporters and punish their enemies. The politicians who are out of power have few alternatives open to them. Maintaining an impersonal civil service is even more difficult. Anonymity is virtually impossible in a small-scale society. Loyalty tends to be partisan loyalty. The civil servant is placed in the dilemma of either becoming a supporter of one party or politician or becoming so cautious that he is trusted by no party and is unable to make effective decisions.

A possible solution to this problem might be found in the city or town manager model used in some American communities. This consists basically of an elected body of councillors hiring an outside administrative expert to carry out the actual administrative tasks of running local government. If a body of such professionals were to be built up, they might be able to provide efficient and impartial administrations for small territories. As an outsider, the manager would not be tied to other inhabitants by personal role-relationships. He would be under a fixed-term contract to the government. He would be bound to implement laws and regulations passed by the legislature. Care would have to be taken to see that he was not a mere creature of the party in power, that he could maintain some independence of action. There would also have to be procedures for removing an inefficient or corrupt manager. His position would be a difficult one. Mauritius is already considering the appointment of an ombudsman to cope with the problem of impartiality. A manager would carry this notion one stage further.

On the basis of this brief survey, are there any 'solutions' for the smaller territories, any ways in which their inhabitants can satisfy their demands for political self-determination and a higher standard of living? It is clear that there is no overall formula which will work for all such territories. Their problems and situations are too diverse for that. Some small territories can exist as separate states because they can take advantage of special requirements of the larger nations. One such requirement is military strategy. Recent history has shown that the needs for bases can change quickly and it would appear that only a few territories can take advantage of this need to the extent that their economies can be supported by the military expenditure of the great powers. Similarly, those few territories which have taken advantage of the restrictions on investment, taxation, or the registration of shipping are vulnerable to changes in these laws by the major powers. Yet a few small territories have existed on this basis for a long time. Hong Kong appears to be a convenience to both China and the West. There seems to be little inclination to infringe on the rights of the Channel Islands. More promising for small territories in the sun is tourism and a haven for the retired. Bermuda and the Bahamas have done very well on this basis, and other West Indian Islands are following suit. As yet, the difficulties and expenses of transportation have prevented the Pacific and Indian Ocean territories from following the same course, but the increasing demand for vacations and retirement in warm climates and the improvement in air services may well bring prosperity to some of these territories. Such developments require the heavy infusion of capital and major changes in the economic and social structure.

Some territories may have to be evacuated. Very small islands, particularly isolated ones in which the able-bodied emigrate, may reach the point of non-viability. Pitcairn has already been mentioned as being very near this point. Tristan da Cunha, St Helena, and the Falkland Islands might also reach this stage.

Another possibility is that some very small islands might become farms or plantations operating a labour force on a seasonal or contract basis. Many of the lesser dependencies of Mauritius and the Seychelles operate in this fashion. The Cocos Islands are a somewhat more permanent plantation. Many of the small islands of the Pacific might lose their permanent populations and become copra plantations.

Wherever possible, the best solution for small territories is to look for some form of economic integration with their neighbours. Small

continental territories close to prosperous neighbours are most favourably placed for this. Here, the model is Luxembourg. Island territories
experience greater difficulties. Often their neighbours are as poor as
themselves. Yet it would appear that economic integration, at least at
this stage of the world's history, is easier to achieve than political
integration.

DEMOGRAPHIC ASPECTS OF SMALLNESS

T. E. Smith

DEMOGRAPHIC CLASSIFICATIONS

Demographically the majority of the smaller countries of the British Commonwealth, dependent and independent, fall into two main categories. The first of these, the larger in number, consists of territories with a fairly dense or very dense population, mostly each of a very few hundred square miles in area (and sometimes much less than one hundred square miles). The second and smaller group consists of countries with an area often running to many thousands of square miles and a population scattered very thinly on the ground. A surprisingly small number of 'smaller territories' are of moderate population density, even if the term 'moderate' is made to cover a wide range. Taking the (1962) Colonial Office List of territories as a base, omitting large countries such as Kenya, and describing a territory as densely peopled if there are more than 250 persons to the square mile and thinly peopled if there are less than 50, the breakdown is as follows:[1]

A *Densely populated* (*More than 250 persons per sq. mile*)	B *Moderate density* (*50–250 persons per sq. mile*)	C *Thinly populated* (*Less than 50 persons per sq. mile*)
Aden (Colony)	Antigua	Aden (Protectorate)
Barbados	Cayman Is.	Bahamas
Bermuda	Dominica	Bechuanaland
Gibraltar	Fiji	(now Botswana)
Grenada	Gambia	British Honduras
Hong Kong	Gilbert & Ellice Is.	Brunei
Jamaica	Basutoland	Falkland Is.
Malta	(now Lesotho)	British Guiana
Mauritius	Nyasaland	(now Guyana)
Montserrat	(now Malawi)	New Hebrides

[1] If we were to consider some of the small Commonwealth countries and territories without relationships with the Colonial Office, Guernsey and Jersey would be in List A, the Isle of Man on the borderline between Lists A and B, and Cyprus definitely in List B. Guernsey, the Isle of Man, and Cyprus have all been losing population in recent years through migration. In the case of Guernsey and the Isle of Man this loss has more than offset the natural increase, i.e. total population is decreasing.

A *Densely populated* (*More than 250 persons* *per sq. mile*)	B *Moderate density* (*50–250 persons* *per sq. mile*)	C *Thinly populated* (*Less than 50 persons* *per sq. mile*)
St Christopher, etc. St Lucia St Vincent Seychelles Singapore Trinidad & Tobago Turks & Caicos Is. Zanzibar	St Helena Tonga Virgin Is.	North Borneo (now Sabah) Sarawak Solomon Is. Swaziland

Lists A and C in the above table differ in characteristics other than
density of population. The majority of the territories in List A have had
a relatively long experience of British administration and were developed either as trading ports or defence bases or for estate production of
a particular crop using imported slave or indentured labour in the early
stages. Very few of the territories in List A had a sizeable population
before the advent of British administration. By contrast a number
(though not all) of the territories in List C have not known the British
as rulers for long, and the present inhabitants are mostly descendants of
people who have inhabited their countries for many generations. Of the
territories in List B, Fiji, St Helena, and the West Indian islands have
more in common with List A, whilst the Gilbert and Ellice Islands,
Tonga, and the African countries of Basutoland, the Gambia and
Nyasaland are more akin to List C.

LIST A TERRITORIES

Population statistics for the territories in List A are on the whole
fairly good. In these compactly sized territories, public health measures
are easier to put into effect than in the larger and more thinly populated
group, and crude death rates are usually low. The transition from high
death rates to low death rates in many of the List A territories has in fact
been quite unusually rapid. Mauritius, Jamaica, and Singapore are three
examples. In Mauritius the crude death rate for most of the years
between the two world wars was between 25 and 30 deaths per thousand population per year; in bad years—e.g. 1930—deaths exceeded
births and in good years the natural increase was usually between 0·5
and 1·0 per cent per annum; in the 1950s, following the eradication of
malaria, the crude death rate ranged between 10·9 and 16·1 and the rate
of natural increase was little short of 3 per cent per annum. In Jamaica
the fall in crude death rates was more gradual—from about 25 just after
World War I to the current rate of about 10; the rate of natural increase

of the Jamaican population is, like that of Mauritius, only marginally below 3 per cent per annum. In Singapore the fall in death rates has been as spectacular as that of Mauritius; as late as the mid-1930s the infant mortality rate was typically between 200 and 300 infant deaths per 1000 live births but the figure is now well under 50: in some of the early years of the century, deaths exceeded births and the population grew rapidly only because of continual immigration, whilst in the 1950s the natural rate of increase of population was amongst the world's highest.

A few of the territories in List A still receive a limited number of immigrants. There has been a very large-scale immigration into Hong Kong since World War II, particularly in the period 1945–55. Over half the residents of Hong Kong at the time of the 1960 census were born outside the territory but the volume of immigration is now much reduced. There is still some immigration into Singapore too—uncontrolled immigration from the Federation of Malaya and controlled immigration from outside Malaya. In general, however, net migratory movement for the List A territories is outwards. In particular, the island territories of the Caribbean, the Indian Ocean, and the Mediterranean export their manpower. Migration to the United Kingdom from Jamaica and other West Indian islands is well documented; the possibility of migration from Jamaica to Africa is under serious examination; there is movement to Trinidad from some of the smaller neighbouring islands, where employment prospects are poor. There are Seychellois in East Africa, Australia, and elsewhere, but accurate information concerning the numbers who have emigrated is not available. About two-thirds of the population of the Cocos Islands in the Indian Ocean were resettled in North Borneo and elsewhere in the early 1950s.

Malta and Gibraltar are two of the few List A island territories for which emigration was on a sufficiently large scale in the 1950s to come close to balancing the excess of births over deaths. Between the 1948 and 1957 censuses the Maltese population grew from 306,000 to only 320,000, despite the fact that the annual excess of births over deaths was nearly 2 per cent of the total population throughout the period; without emigration the population would have grown by about 6,000 per year. More than half the emigrants in 1960 (Malta, *Demographic Review*, 1960) went to Australia (2,304 out of 3,841); substantial numbers went to the United Kingdom (878) and Canada (509), and a smaller batch to the U.S.A. In 1954, the year of peak emigration, 8,470 out of a total of 11,447 emigrants went to Australia. On a much smaller scale, the excess (1,792) of births over deaths in Gibraltar between 1951 and 1961 was nearly balanced by the emigration of 1,671 people in the decade.

Migration to the United Kingdom has gone far in recent years to match natural increase in Jamaica. The figures (Jamaica, *Quarterly Abstract of Statistics*, 1962) for natural increase and migration to the United Kingdom in the three years 1959–61 were:

Year	Excess of births over deaths	Migrants to the U.K. less migrants returning
1959	48,104	10,478
1960	54,845	30,269
1961	52,569	37,615
1st Qr. 1962	13,508	7,349

Barbados had a population density of over 1,000 persons to the square mile as far back as the late nineteenth century and Barbadians have for long looked to emigration as the only method of easing their island's population problem. At different times, Barbadian labour has found employment opportunities in the Canal Zone, Cuba, Costa Rica, Panama, British Guiana, Trinidad, and elsewhere, and the population of Barbados at the time of the 1921 census was considerably smaller than in 1896. Since 1921, however, population has grown slowly though current emigration still restricts the rate of increase to under one per cent per annum. The 1960 census population was 232,000 compared with 186,000 in 1896 and 166,000 in 1921.

The effect of migration on population growth in the Caribbean area generally can be gauged from the following figures taken from the 1961 U.N. Demographic Year Book:

I Territory	II Average annual rate of increase of population 1953–60 %	III Natural rate of increase 1960 %
1 *Commonwealth*		
Bahamas	3·0	2·4
British Honduras	2·9	3·7
Antigua	1·6	2·2
Barbados	0·7	2·3
Dominica	0·5	3·2
Grenada	0·9	3·4
Jamaica	1·2	3·4
Montserrat	−1·6	1·8
St Kitts–Nevis	1·4	2·8
St Lucia	0·4	3·1
St Vincent	1·5	3·5
Trinidad & Tobago	3·2	2·6 (1961 figure)
Turks & Caicos Is.	−2·8	?

II *Non-Commonwealth*		
Cuba	2·1	2·1
Guadeloupe	2·8	2·9
Martinique	2·4	2·9

Where the figure in the third column is appreciably higher than the figure in the second column, as it is for most of the Commonwealth territories but not for the non-Commonwealth areas quoted, there is certainly a good deal of net emigration and, as can be seen, this has been sufficient in the case of Montserrat and the Turks and Caicos Islands to lead to an actual reduction of population during the 1950s.

For Mauritius, Titmuss and Abel-Smith consider that 'To assume that the problem of over-population can be overcome by emigration is no more than wishful thinking . . . Quite apart from the difficulty of finding countries willing to accept Mauritians on the scale and at the speed that would be necessary, there are the heavy costs of training and transport . . .' (1960, p. 238). The annual increment to the population of Mauritius (numbering about 649,000 in 1960) is now approaching 20,000. The density of population exceeds 900 persons to the square mile—a very high density indeed for an agricultural country; this density compares closely with that of Holland and exceeds that of Belgium, though it is not as high as that of Barbados in the West Indies.

Some of the territories in List A greatly exceed Mauritius in density of population, but the population problems may nevertheless not be quite so intractable. For instance, Singapore, with a population of 7,500 on the average in each of its 225 square miles, is the New York of Malaysia (and Kuala Lumpur its Washington); the growth of Singapore is simply a part of the world history of urbanization.[1] Again, Hong Kong, with its 8,000 people to the square mile, is geographically part of China, whatever its future political status, and rapid industrialization has absorbed most of the post-war wave of refugee immigration. In both these city states birth-control campaigns are beginning to have their effect on birth rates; in Singapore, where birth and death registration statistics are reliable, the annual total of births has declined slowly since 1958, and the rate of decline appears to be accelerating.[2]

Most of the List A territories are, however, still in the second phase of the demographic revolution—i.e. the phase in which the death rate is falling and the birth rate is more or less constant.

[1] The growth of population in the whole Malaysian area is, however, far too rapid for economic comfort.
[2] The figures for 1958, 1959, 1960, and 1961 were 62,495, 62,464, 61,775, and 59,930. In the first four months of 1962 the number was 18,824 against 19,222 in the first four months of 1961. In the meantime the natural increase in population per annum is about 50,000.

The typical age structure of a List A territory is, of course, that of a high fertility population. Given a stable population unaffected by migration, it is the level of fertility (rather than the level of mortality) which is the primary determinant of age structure. Given high fertility, both a high mortality and a low mortality population will have some 40 per cent of its population under the age of 15. Thus, in Mauritius, which has a high birth rate but little emigration, the age structure of the population in 1931 (high death rate period) and 1952 (low death rate period) was as follows:

Age-group	1931 % in group	1952 % in group
Under 15	38·4	40·8
15–64	58·7	56·3
65 and over	2·9	2·9

These figures should be contrasted with the position in Western Europe where the proportion of under 15s is only one quarter of the population or less, and the proportion of the people of working age (15–64) is some two-thirds of the total population.

As we have seen, migration is in fact a matter of great social and economic importance in many of the List A territories and, in so far as groups of emigrants usually contain a large proportion of young adults, the percentage of people of working age will be still further reduced. This can be illustrated from the results of three successive censuses (1931, 1948, and 1957) of Malta, whose population has a medium rather than a high birth rate. The percentages are as follows:

Age-group	1931 Male	Female	1948 Male	Female	1957 Male	Female
Under 15	33·6	31·0	36·0	34·2	39·9	35·4
15–64	60·8	63·3	59·1	60·3	53·9	57·8
65 and over	5·6	5·6	4·9	5·5	6·1	6·7

Post-war emigration has had the effect of reducing the percentage of adults of working age, particularly for the male population. A combination of really high fertility and substantial emigration of young adults in any community could well have the effect of reducing the working population to less than half of the total.

In List A there is one territory—Bermuda—with a demographic character somewhat unlike that of the rest. Bermuda is a haven for wealthy persons of middle age who require a place of residence with a warm climate and low rates of taxation. In these circumstances it is not surprising to find that the percentage of the Bermudan population over

45 years of age, at 21·9 per cent in 1960, is higher than in other colonial territories, though low in relation to some other small territory tax-havens such as Monaco and the Channel Islands. The crude birth rate is fairly high (32·4 per 1000 population) for the coloured population, who are mainly Bermudans by birth, but the birth rate of the white population is low.

To sum up, the List A territories consist broadly of two distinct groups:

(a) Largely urban territories of very small area which are linked economically with one or more surrounding countries. In some cases population is still flowing into these territories as part of the process of urbanization.

(b) Territories usually consisting of one or more islands, which are mostly dependent economically on the specialized production of crops for export. The population of these territories has often grown in past years through labour immigration, but the movement of population is now generally outward.

Finding a home for surplus population is, in fact, often as important to small territories as finding a market for their crops and manufactures. Those territories which do succeed in finding a home for surplus population must face the fact that they will retain an excessively high proportion of people who are too young or too old to work. Some of these territories have established migratory links (though the doors of the receiving country may not necessarily remain open), whilst others such as Mauritius must either reduce the rate of growth of population or face disaster.

LIST C TERRITORIES

The territories in List C include some of the most undeveloped areas in the British Commonwealth. Most of these territories contain a high proportion of jungle or desert, and development has been restricted largely to areas contiguous to the main town or towns.

In some of these territories, immigration has in the past been the main source of population growth. Thus, in British Guiana, the increase in population up to 1911 was entirely due to immigration, mortality rates being so high that the contribution from natural increase was very small indeed. Indeed, for some years of the period 1911–1921, deaths exceeded births. Since 1921, however, there has been no large immigration but natural increase has emerged as the important growth factor. Migration records in fact suggest that in the past two or three decades the balance of movement has been outwards, and this has been accompanied by a growing concentration of population in and around Georgetown. The results of the 1946 census of British Guiana showed a net migrational loss of population from almost all the rural areas of the colony.

A far higher percentage of the population of British Guiana are the descendants of immigrants than is the case for most of the other List C territories. In North Borneo and Sarawak, the immigrant Chinese, nearly a quarter in the former and a third in the latter, are economically the most important section of the population but the indigenous peoples outnumber them; in these two territories, as in Fiji in List B, the rate of natural increase of the immigrant group far exceeds that of the indigenous group. Indeed the rate of growth of the *indigenous* population is in general lower throughout the List C territories than is that of the general population in the List A territories. Whereas the rate of natural increase of the typical List A territory approaches 3 per cent per annum, the rate for the indigenous population of the typical List C territory probably falls short of 2 per cent; it must be stated here, however, that demographic statistics (in so far as they exist) for some of the List C territories —e.g. Aden Protectorate, the Solomon Islands, and Bechuanaland— are far from reliable.

Despite their emptiness and the relatively low rate of growth of population, some of the List C territories export their man-power. Many thousands of labourers from the High Commission Territories work in South Africa. The net movement of population is outwards from isolated islands like the Falkland Islands and St Helena (the latter in List B[1]). On the other hand, there is now no sizeable immigrant movement into any of the List C territories.

LIST B TERRITORIES

In an article on the population of the main island groups of Polynesia (1961), Dr Norma McArthur demonstrated that the average annual rate of growth of the populations of Fiji, Western Samoa, American Samoa, Tonga, Cook Islands, and French Polynesia were in every case over 3 per cent in the period 1956–61 and that the average annual rates of growth of the labour forces were in excess of the rates of growth of the population as a whole. Of these territories, only American Samoa and the Cook Islands could hope to have their problems solved by emigration. Dr McArthur concluded her article with this paragraph:

The inevitable and rapid increase in labour potential is the crucial factor for all these populations. Agriculture as practised at present cannot support the same or an even higher proportion of the total work force and somehow alternative means of livelihood must be created and then expanded continuously if the

[1] There has been a regular emigration of St Helenians to the United Kingdom, mainly to work as domestic servants.

present standards are to be maintained. The regular and continuing expansion of employment opportunities at rates ranging from 3 to $4\frac{1}{2}$ per cent per year will not be easy, especially for those populations where agricultural expansion is blocked by limited land resources, or traditional systems of land tenure, or difficulties in the marketing of agricultural produce. The drift of young males away from rural environments will aggravate the employment situation in urban areas and increasing urbanization without sufficient economic basis will have far-reaching social consequences which, in the long run, may prove more costly to governments than the initiation of realistic programmes of development designed to promote the economic and social well-being of the people for whom they are responsible.

The position of Nyasaland and Basutoland is quite unlike that of Fiji and Tonga in relation to opportunities for their respective labour forces. Despite Dr Banda's attitude towards white-dominated governments, the men of Nyasaland continued in 1961 to stream out of their own country and into the Rhodesias and South Africa in search of work, any reduction in the numbers going to Southern Rhodesia as the result of unemployment in that country being counter-balanced by an increased recruitment for work in the mines of South Africa. Similarly Basutoland continues to rely on South Africa for employment opportunities for its males of working age. Moreover, the rate of natural increase of the population of the two African countries is lower than that of Fiji and Tonga.

The West Indian territories of Antigua and Dominica in List B have, as has been seen in the discussion on List A, been able to offset their high rate of natural increase with some migration.

SMALL COUNTRIES AND TERRITORIES OTHER THAN THOSE INCLUDED IN THE 1962 COLONIAL OFFICE LIST

Whatever the precise standard of smallness, small countries and territories not included in the 1962 Colonial Office List, whether in the Commonwealth or outside it, have a wide range in political and economic standing. Included in my tentative list are countries and territories as diverse as French Somaliland, Panama, Andorra, Macao, Surinam, and the Isle of Man. The list nevertheless shares with the Colonial Office List a definite preponderance of small countries with a high population density; the high density countries include Réunion in the Indian Ocean, whose problems may be similar to those of Mauritius; the former Trust territory of Ruanda-Urundi, which must surely continue to rely on emigration to Uganda and other neighbouring African countries; Israel, whose density of population is already as great as that of Northern Ireland and whose continued population growth is due as much to immigration as to natural increase; the small Caribbean territories of Martinique and Guadeloupe under French administration, and Curaçao and other neighbouring islands under Dutch administration; the European countries of Liechtenstein, Luxembourg, and Monaco; the Spanish cities of Ceuta and Melilla in North Africa; and the oil island of Bahrein. This list is far from exhaustive, but all share the characteristic of having a population density of over 250 persons to the square mile.

There is, however, a great diversity within these countries in rates of population growth. Broadly speaking, the small countries and territories outside the tropics, most of which are culturally European, have low rates of natural increase. In such countries the demographic revolution is nearly complete and birth rates and death rates are nearly equal at a low level. The rate of natural increase of Luxembourg, for instance, is as low or lower than that of the United Kingdom (the United Kingdom rate is just over 0·5 per cent per annum) and the rates for Ceuta and Melilla compare fairly closely with that of Spain (1·3 per cent per annum). Within the tropics, however, birth rates and rates of natural increase are high—the latter rates are over 3 per cent per annum in Réunion and Ruanda-Urundi, and not far short of 3 per cent in Guadeloupe.

In the densely populated tropical small countries outside the Commonwealth, as within it, the basic demographic problem revolves around the opportunity for surplus labour to emigrate. The development of oil refineries in Curaçao and Aruba temporarily solved the problems of the smaller islands in the Netherlands Antilles, such as Bonaire and St Maarten, and the years between the world wars in fact saw a drop in the population of these smaller islands whilst industrialization has led to Curaçao's numbers being multiplied fourfold and Aruba's population multiplied sevenfold between 1920 and 1960. This spate of growth in the population of the two major islands has now, however, ended and latest estimates suggest that the emphasis has switched to emigration.

The lightly populated small countries outside the Commonwealth are in large part colonial territories or departments of France, the Netherlands, and Portugal, situated in Africa and South America. The Danish territory of Greenland, the oil state of Kuwait, and the Republic of Panama are other countries which are both small and enter the low-density category.

GENERAL CONSIDERATIONS

It is clear that emigration often plays a far more important part in the social and economic life of small densely populated countries such as Jamaica, Barbados, and Malta than in large densely populated countries such as India and China. Emigration from the latter countries could never be on a large enough scale to have any real effect on the net rate of population growth. A high rate of migration (whether immigration or emigration) as a percentage of total population is not, however, an essential ingredient of smallness, nor are countries which do receive or dispatch a large number of migrants in relation to the total population necessarily small.[1]

The continuation of some kind of colonial link with a metropolitan power does not ensure migratory outlets for surplus population, nor does such a link ensure that low-density small countries will receive the population (and capital and skills) needed for development. As a case study of this truism, the abandoned project of emigration from over-crowded Mauritius to under-populated North Borneo is of some interest. In 1949 the Labour Commissioner of Mauritius undertook a detailed study of the possibilities of labour migration from Mauritius to Borneo and recommended that a small group should be settled on an European-owned tobacco plantation as an initial venture (Wilkinson, 1949). No action was ultimately taken on the recommendation. In the first place, employers in North Borneo have always complained in a general way of the shortage of labour but have been reluctant to pay for its import; it was the question of costs which put paid to ideas of Indian immigration into Borneo in the early 1950s, though on that occasion the costs would have been paid by the Government rather than by individual employers. At the Mauritian end, North Borneo was envisaged as a country in which 'the climate is hot and damp, conditions are primitive and the country has a long way to go before its amenities reach the standard of those in Mauritius'. In the circumstances it is hardly surprising that the prospect of migration to Borneo seemed insufficiently encouraging to be worth pursuing.

A somewhat similar story could be told of the position of British Guiana and British Honduras *vis-à-vis* the British West Indies. '. . . Resettlement in these two colonies would mean, for the most part, resettlement in country hitherto wholly undeveloped and unsettled, and in many cases even unexplored. Apart from the heavy capital expenditures involved in the way of opening up the interior by means of roads, railways and air services, and the organization required to provide all the essential services, such as schools, housing, water supply; medical services, and the like, the prospective immigrants would be arriving without capital equipment, or the skilled knowledge necessary' (Proudfoot, 1950, pp. 25–6). No wonder that the relatively civilized conditions of living in Trinidad and the United Kingdom have

[1] A glance at the history of immigration into the United States and Australia and of emigration from Italy and Ireland is proof enough on this point.

had a greater attractive power for British West Indians. No wonder too that the government-sponsored experiment of resettling groups from Barbados and St Lucia in the Dutch colony of Surinam proved a failure—the workers complaining of low wages and poor living conditions and the Surinam Government complaining that the men could not do the work required of them and that the groups of migrants were more trouble than they were ever likely to be worth.

The solution to the population problems of small countries is far from obvious. The lightly peopled small countries which need more population as one of a number of conditions for economic development can find little comfort in the world tendency for people to concentrate more and more in urban and industrial communities. The densely peopled small countries with non-European populations find the doors of other countries increasingly difficult to open. In many such countries, it is still only a small minority of the people who are aware of the significance of the rapid growth of population, and often birth control campaigns run counter both to religious opinion and to entrenched patterns of behaviour. In territories which remain colonial and whose population has been built up by labour immigration as a deliberate policy of the metropolitan power, it seems to me that the metropolitan power retains a continuing responsibility to assist in social, economic and political development—a responsibility of a rather different order compared with its responsibility in larger countries containing indigenous populations for whom colonial rule is merely a passing phase.

2

THE SMALLER TERRITORIES:
SOME POLITICAL CONSIDERATIONS

D. P. J. Wood

Even in the late 1950s it was still possible to imagine that a rough rule of thumb existed to make a distinction, in political terms at least, between the larger and smaller dependencies within the Commonwealth. It seemed then that there were certain yardsticks of statehood to determine whether a colony would ever gain full independence in its own right. Ideally there had to be some political expertise, an administration to carry on more or less effectively when the new state had to shoulder its own responsibilities, a feeling of national unity which would survive the enthusiasms of the first months of independence and a reasonable economic framework. To be financially viable, the local revenue had to be able to cope with new burdens, such as diplomacy and armed forces, as well as its accustomed current expenses. To be politically viable, the dominant parties should have to say more than 'Massa day done'. The dependencies which looked unlikely to become fully independent were in some sense or other undoubtedly 'small' whether in area or population or resources, or in a combination of all three, when compared with the then independent countries in the Commonwealth.

But by their nature rules of thumb are approximate and flexible; this particular one, which never hardened by open official expression into a dogma, proved to be particularly outmoded and loose. Independence was granted to countries which by reason of their size or prevailing notions of economic and political maturity seemed unsuited to its demands, and small territories which had already been grouped into federations for their well-being broke away to stand on their own feet. Those who thought about the political future of the rump of the colonial empire left one overriding consideration out of their reckoning. The demand for sovereignty could be as urgent and strong among the politically conscious in the smaller territories as in the larger; they were in no way abashed by the difficulties that freedom might bring. In 1957 and 1958, for instance, the Labour Party and the Conservative Political Centre published pamphlets on the smaller territories (Labour Party, 1957; Blood, 1958). Their authors believed that full sovereignty was not possible for the great majority of the colonies of the time. Even

Sierra Leone was considered a borderline case. Yet from 1959 until 1965 not only Sierra Leone but also Cyprus, Jamaica, Trinidad, Nyasaland (Malawi), Malta (approximately the size of the British sovereign bases in Cyprus), Zanzibar, and the Gambia achieved full independence. The sights have been lowered and today it is impossible to tell how far and how fast the process of decolonization will go on. What may be called the sound barrier of smallness has been broken and the only certainty in a confused situation is that decolonization will continue. No one can predict the limiting instance or in what forms independence will appear.

Some smaller territories have moved along the path to independence in recent years through federations. For a long time they have been a favourite device of constitutional fathers in the Commonwealth. In different forms they exist in Canada (1867), Australia (1901), Malaya (1948), India (1950), and Nigeria (1960). Federations are a tempting solution because they may produce a viable entity out of poor and struggling constituents and perhaps there is also the rather cynical inducement of killing, as it were, seven with one blow. On the other hand there are dangers and the smaller territories have encountered them in full measure. As time goes on the partners in the union may find themselves increasingly at loggerheads and finally irreconcilable. Two federations of the 1950s, Rhodesia and Nyasaland and the West Indies, in which there had been comparatively little contact between the members, much diversity in wealth, population and resources, and varying degrees of enthusiasm for the link among both politicians and people, have already disintegrated. Neighbouring states may claim that the federation is a threat to their integrity and merely a neo-colonial manipulation by Britain to retain some control. And surely the comment of the calypsonian, the Mighty Sparrow, on the failing Federation of the West Indies is of more general application in the conditions of the mid-twentieth century:

> Federation boil down to simply this,
> It's dog-eat-dog and survival of the fittest.
> Everybody going for independence
> Singularly.
> Trinidad, for instance,
> And we'll get it too, boy, don't bother. (James, n.d., p. 167.)

In March 1963 Aden acceded to the Federation of Southern Arabia which at that time consisted of eleven autonomous states in the Western Protectorate. The relevant treaty recognized the strategic importance of the colony by reserving to the Government of the United Kingdom the power to exclude or to withdraw at any time those areas in Aden itself which it considered necessary for its defence responsibilities.

The authority of the Governor prevails over that of the Federation government in Aden itself on matters of defence, security, and external affairs (G.B., Cmnd. 1814, 1962). This provokes accusations of neo-colonialism from Moscow, San'a, and Cairo alike, and in Aden itself there is opposition inside the Legislative Assembly and violence in the streets against the link with backward states whose inhabitants have no political voice and whose autocratic rulers outnumber the representatives of Aden in the Federal Council by three to one. The whole issue is complicated by Yemeni claims that the protectorates are legally part of South Yemen.

The passage of the most recent federation has been equally stormy. In September 1963 Malaysia was created from the existing independent Federation of Malaya and the remaining colonies of Britain in Southeast Asia, Singapore, North Borneo, and Sarawak. They already shared a currency and a *lingua franca*, Singapore was their common entrepôt, and each had experienced for varying lengths of time the moulding influences of British colonial administration. In spite of some fears in the politically inexperienced Borneo territories that the known British colonialism might be exchanged for unknown Malayan domination and that racial tensions between the Chinese and the indigenous peoples throughout the new Federation might be exacerbated, the new Federation had much to commend it (T. E. Smith, 1962). There seemed no promising alternative for the two Borneo territories except perhaps some closer union between themselves and the protected State of Brunei which decided not to join the Federation during the final negotiations on Malaysia in July 1963. But Indonesian hostility threatens the stability of the Federation of Malaysia as much as the internal dissensions which caused Singapore to leave the Federation in August 1965.

One other federation of smaller territories was planned. The East Caribbean Federation Conference held in London in May 1962 proposed a federation of Barbados and the Windward and Leeward Islands with ultimately full independence within the Commonwealth (G.B., Cmnd. 1746, 1962). Without Jamaica and Trinidad this proposed federation would have been but a pale ghost of the defunct Federation of the West Indies and would have been still further weakened by the desire of Grenada to join Trinidad in a unitary state. This attempt to federate proved abortive. Antigua withdrew from the protracted and inconclusive discussions in 1965 and the Government of Barbados announced that it wanted separate independence before considering federation further. The British Government as a second best proposed that the islands of the Windwards and Leewards (with the exception of Montserrat) should become states in association with Britain. Each should have control of its internal affairs and the right to amend its own constitution, including the power to end unilaterally the association with Britain. The British Government for its part would accept responsibility for their external relations and defence. Talks were held in the first half of 1966 and these proposals for a new form of post-colonial relationship met with a favourable response from the islands. The British Virgin Islands which were never in the former federation, the Turks and Caicos Islands, and the Caymans, dependencies of Jamaica until 1959 when they were constituted separate colonies, will still be left as British territories in the Caribbean. Even if the American and British Virgin Islands were to integrate, the problem of their future status would hardly be solved.

A mention has been made of Grenada's wish to integrate with Trinidad and this solution has already been tried elsewhere. British Somaliland and the Italian Trust Territory of Somalia integrated in July 1960 to form the independent Somali Republic. The consciousness of a common kinship was strong on both sides of the border and the people were convinced that their political and economic advancement would only be fostered by union. A few months later, in February 1961, the British Trust Territory of the Northern Cameroons voted in a United Nations plebiscite to be incorporated into Nigeria, and it is now the Sardauna province in the Northern Region. At the same time the Southern Cameroons elected to join the already independent French-speaking Republic of Cameroun to form the Federal Republic of Cameroon. In the south the decision was harder to make than in the north where the inhabitants had close ethnic ties over the Nigerian border. Opinion in the Southern Cameroons had been divided for some time between those who wanted a merger with Nigeria and those who supported the 'Kamerun idea'; the issue between them was not finally resolved until the plebiscite (Ardener, 1962).

On the other side of Africa the complex process of integration began with far less warning and public discussion when Zanzibar merged with Tanganyika in 1964. The Republic of Tanzania is the only instance of two emerging countries in the Commonwealth integrating after they had achieved independence separately. Elsewhere in the world there seems little chance of integration, either sudden or slow, as a solution to the political and economic problems of small territories although there have been discussions of this for the enclave of the Gambia, formerly the smallest British dependency on the west coast of Africa.

In February 1965 the Gambia became the twenty-first member of the Commonwealth and the thirty-sixth independent African state. At first sight integration with Senegal is an attractive geographical solution. The Gambia river is navigable for 300 miles (the whole length of the former protectorate) for vessels drawing six feet of water and it would provide cheap and easy communications with its natural hinterland of Senegal. The economic development of Senegal and Mali has been retarded by this unnatural divorce from one of the finest and safest of African rivers. Yet there are snags to the creation of Senegambia. Unlike the Horn of Africa, for instance, the two countries have been moulded by a long period of different colonial rule. Modern Senegal is very much a country *d'expression française*; the Gambia on the other hand had been a British colony since 1843. In spite of common tribal and even family affinities with the Senegalese, the influential Gambian chiefs fear the loss of their power if integration comes about. In both countries there have been misgivings about the relationship and even rivalry between the port of Dakar and the potentialities of the Gambia river. Moreover the Gambia is far less developed than Senegal, and the prospect of having to bolster up its economy, while attempting at the same time to improve their own makes the elite of Senegal cautious (Welch, 1962, p. 1417; *West Africa*, 1965).

Other small territories which appear to the outsider even less well endowed for independence than those already discussed are nonetheless moving towards it. In the Indian Ocean, for example, party politics began in the Seychelles in June 1963 when the Seychelles Islanders' United Party was formed to oppose the longer established Taxpayers' and Producers' Association. An inconclusive constitutional conference has already been held to decide the way of Mauritius to independence.

For some dependencies their size and geographical remoteness make independence either on their own or by integration or in a federation seem unlikely. All that they can hope for and indeed all that they probably want is the greatest possible degree of self-government with links either with the metropolitan power or a nearer Commonwealth country. A precedent has been set for a form of clientship which may well be a pattern elsewhere. The New Zealand Trust Territory of Western Samoa became the first fully independent Polynesian state on 1 January 1962. New Zealand conducts the foreign affairs of Western Samoa, such as they are, through its own diplomatists. But no one can say what would happen if at some future time the interests of both were to diverge. In Lesotho there were before independence suggestions that, to help resolve the dilemma of wanting independence which black African countries see as their birthright and also needing influential protection from their large neighbour, relations similar to those which Britain has with oil sheikhdoms in the Persian Gulf might be worked out. And as the Commonwealth grows larger there may be room for smaller regional groupings within it for the discussion of issues which may not concern all members, and herein may lie the germ of new associations.

Yet it would be idle to pretend that the implications of clientship of various kinds have been thought out or that it would be possible to ward off accusations of neo-colonialism and spheres of interest among those jealous of their liberty. In the middle of the twentieth century it is easier and less humiliating to accept foreign economic aid and technical advice than overseas political guidance and skills. In addition some smaller territories may be able to satisfy their political aspirations by joining a regional economic community which might strengthen their economies without any suspicion of neo-colonialism and without a great diminution of their sovereignty. The pace is being set in the Americas. In the last few years study groups have been at work in Trinidad and Surinam to see if the foundations can be laid for a Caribbean Common Market which would transcend former colonial boundaries. Surinam is part of the United Kingdom of the Netherlands and an associate member of E.E.C. If the intricate legal and economic problems contained in these relationships can be worked out there may be a precedent not only for the British islands but for the Netherlands and French Antilles as well.

It is one of the paradoxes of the age that while great powers are getting greater, more and more independent countries are appearing that in economic strength and population scarcely measure up to an American state or even an English county. The world moves into a situation for which there are no concepts, where there is more and more independence and interdependence, and where traditional notions of sovereignty are being eroded. Countries give up with varying degrees of reluctance some sovereignty to the United Nations. International civil servants and soldiers under the orders of the United Nations attempt to settle the internal dissensions of member states. Regional economic and defensive alliances may imply a radical renunciation of national sovereignty to some supra-national entity in the future. Even for the United States and the Soviet Union complete freedom of action is an illusion; many medium and small powers are bound to a larger ally; the developing countries have to live and seek aid in a world in which two great international systems compete and in which it sometimes pays them to bluster and sometimes to woo, sometimes to remain uncommitted and sometimes to take sides.

Such general considerations complicate the problem of independence and sovereignty for all emerging countries. It becomes increasingly difficult to define these ideas, and for small territories other inhibiting factors exist which seem to have something to do with their size.

No attempt has been made so far in this discussion to define smallness. The smaller territories of the Commonwealth, whether independent or not, have only one apparent general characteristic and that is diversity.

They vary in resources, population, their degree of economic and
political development, and area. They are to be found in every ocean
except the Arctic and in every continent except Australia. Some are
part of a large land mass: others are scattered through an archipelago;
others again are solitary islands separated from their nearest neighbours
by hundreds of miles of sea. In size they range from about two square
miles (Gibraltar and Pitcairn) to approximately 500,000 square miles
(the Falkland Islands dependencies). The population of Hong Kong is
at least three million but the Central and Southern Islands in the Pacific
are usually uninhabited and it is impossible to speak in the same breath
of the free port of Hong Kong (whose exports and re-exports in 1963
exceeded in value those of Pakistan, Ceylon, Ghana, and Nigeria) and
Pitcairn Island whose main export is postage stamps.[1]

Moreover the political pressures to which the smaller territories are
subjected are as varied. As an example, consider the implications of the
frontier between Lesotho (39 square miles larger than Belgium) and
South Africa on the one hand and that between Gibraltar and Spain on
the other. If in a figurative sense, as Miss Wallman put it in the seminar
(See Appendix, p. 149), Lesotho is a dormitory suburb of the Transvaal, in a more literal way the southern fringes of the Spanish province
of Cadiz are a dormitory suburb of Gibraltar. The two larger countries
have political claims over their smaller neighbours but the economic
roles of great to small are opposite in each relationship. And it is hard to
point to a more striking difference than that between the lax frontiers
of the British and American Virgin Islands and the rigid frontier between Hong Kong and China. It is easy to find other examples. The
combinations of circumstances determining the present and future condition of the smaller territories are as numerous as the countries themselves.

Because of these considerations it proved impossible for the seminar
to decide what 'smallness' means with any precision. It is a comparative
and not an absolute idea. Whatever scales of magnitude are employed
seem arbitrary and it is difficult to pick out on them where smallness
begins or ends. Countries can be small in one sense and not in another.
Smallness in whatever form it may exist is only one of the variables.
The issue is complicated still further by the significant factor of remoteness, whether simple geographical remoteness or remoteness from
the intellectual mainstreams of the world.

Remoteness may, for instance, make economic integration or even

[1] Value of Exports and Re-exports (£ million) 1963: Hong Kong £312, Pakistan £149, Ceylon £128, Ghana £97, Nigeria £190. (*Commonwealth Trade 1963*.
London, H.M.S.O. for the Commonwealth Economic Committee, 1964, Table 1,
p. 88.)

co-operation with a larger state inconceivable and this in its turn may hamper political development. The Isle of Man enjoys an almost full measure of political independence, due to a great extent to its close economic ties with Britain; it would be in a sad plight if it were isolated in an unfrequented ocean instead of being in the enclosed Irish Sea.

In the uncertain and changing field of strategy remoteness may be one of the factors that influence the political and economic future of smaller territories. Geopolitics and defence requirements change with time. Antigua and Jamaica have probably sunk into strategic insignificance; St Helena in the constant south-east trade winds lost its naval importance with the rise of steam navigation but it may regain this if Simonstown is denied to the Royal Navy; the Falkland Islands, valuable in two world wars, may become supremely important if the Panama Canal is destroyed by a nuclear attack. And because of its remoteness and the circulation of the winds in its upper atmosphere Christmas Island was the main nuclear testing ground in the Commonwealth. Other islands in the Indian or Pacific Oceans may become strategically useful as air staging posts if the more conventional air routes to Australia and the Far East over the Middle East, Africa, and Southern Asia are forbidden to military aircraft. But it is impossible to assess the strategic factors with any precision. The defence appraisals and overseas commitments of Britain are in a state of flux and it is hard to know which smaller territories are or will be important. There is a further consideration as well. As the range of aircraft and ships increase and armies become ever more mobile, the need for strategically sited bases in the sensitive areas in the world for repairs, refuelling, and static garrisons diminishes until all that may be left in the future is a stockpile of heavy equipment guarded by a handful of second line soldiers. This does not irrigate the economy in the way that an established garrison does and even stockpiles may vanish as Britain withdraws more and more from its old imperial role.

Another external factor complicates the future of some smaller territories. Foreign countries have historical claims on them. A mention has already been made of Yemeni demands for the Adenese Protectorates; elsewhere too there are irredenta.

As early as 1820 the Captaincy-General of Buenos Aires first claimed sovereignty over the Falklands, and the assertion of *de jure* sovereignty has never been given up by its heir, the Argentine Republic (Ferns, 1960, pp. 225–33). During and after the Second World War the strategic, scientific, and possible economic value of Antarctica became increasingly apparent. The Argentine stepped up its claims for the Falkland Islands Dependencies (South Georgia, South Orkneys, South

Shetlands, South Sandwich Islands, and Graham Land) and the British sector of continental Antarctica itself. Both the Argentine and Chile (whose territorial claims conflicted in part with those of the Argentine) set up bases in the British sector and these were countered by token British settlements. The story became more serious when the Soviet Union claimed the right to participate in any discussion on the political future of the region on commercial grounds (e.g. whaling) and historical grounds (e.g. the work of early nineteenth-century explorers such as Bellinghausen). Antarctica and the British dependencies within it were drawn into power politics in the 1950s;[1] but in 1959 the Treaty of Washington between the twelve nations then engaged in scientific research put the claims and counterclaims into cold storage and banned new ones in the area south of 60°S. Yet South Georgia, the South Sandwich group, and the Falklands themselves lie north of this latitude and the Argentine can bring up its claim to these territories whenever it thinks fit.

Also with its roots in the disintegration of the Spanish Empire in the Americas is the complicated and long-lived controversy over the Guatemalan claim to sovereignty over British Honduras.[2] This dispute has never been submitted to international arbitration because of objections raised sometimes by the United Kingdom and sometimes by Guatemala. At one time the premier of British Honduras, Mr George Price, advocated close ties, if not union, with Guatemala. He was even expelled from the Executive Council in 1957 for alleged secret negotiations at the Guatemalan Legation during constitutional talks in London (Waddell, *infra*, p. 66). But Guatemala overplayed its hand; British Hondurans were affronted in the early 1960s by raids across the border and Mr Price and his party, the People's United Party, rejected the demands of the Guatemalans for the incorporation of the colony. They now campaign for full independence with economic links with the republics of Central America. The tense atmosphere has relaxed after talks in Puerto Rico in 1962 between representatives of British Honduras, Guatemala, and the United Kingdom.

Space does not permit more than a brief reference to other irredenta. In Europe Spain sporadically campaigns for Gibraltar and on the opposite flank of the Eurasian land mass the embarrassing prospect exists that China will demand Hong Kong Island itself (ceded in perpetuity to Britain in 1842) when the lease of the New Territories expires at the end of this century. One way that the Philippines can exert—and have

[1] *v.* G. C. L. Bertram, 'Antarctic Prospect', *International Affairs*, vol. xxxiii, no. 2, 1957, for a survey of the various claims to segments of Antarctica.
[2] For the history of this dispute *v.* R. A. Humphreys, *The Diplomatic History of British Honduras, 1638–1901*, London, 1961.

exerted—pressure on Malaysia is by arguing that the Sultan of Sulu, whose descendants are now Filippino subjects, only leased, not ceded, his territories on the East Coast of Sabah to Britain in 1878. South Africa, both as a Dominion and a Republic, has looked to the High Commission Territories; their incorporation would be invaluable for the full implementation of the Bantustan policies.

In these territories however no significant proportion of the inhabitants support the irredentist claims. There is no fervour for Enosis as in Cyprus. In some of them a majority are racially or linguistically different from their would-be liberators (Falkland Islands, British Honduras, Sabah); in others the people feel that their freedom or standards of living would be in jeopardy (Gibraltar, Hong Kong). As Britain relinquishes more and more of her imperial responsibilities and her power in the world becomes ever weaker these irredenta, however, may well become serious external threats to some of the smaller territories. Because of their size the demands of relatively weak neighbours could take on the potency of an ultimatum. It would be the more effective by being cloaked in an appeal to uncommitted outsiders that yet another injustice of the age of European colonization was being redressed.

Smallness, however elusive and hard to define, is one of the key factors in such a situation because it does seem that to be at the low end of the scale of nations means a vulnerability to crises and pressures that larger countries can shrug off or overcome. There are also hazards lurking in the geography and demography of smallness; weaknesses may appear in the social and economic structure and their effects can ruin the best laid plans and cast terrible burdens on the government whether colonial or autonomous. No typhoon on the Japanese coast, for example, compares in gravity with the full force of a hurricane striking a small West Indian island. It is the difference between a limited and general calamity; in the one instance the whole population is involved in circumstances of misery and destitution, in the other only part of the community suffers and life goes on normally for the majority. Important sectors of the economy remain unscathed or are even stimulated by the distress of the minority.

Again it is generally true that the smaller the country, the more limited are its natural resources. This may not be disadvantageous if its products are eagerly sought by the world, as sugar and spices were in the past and oil is today. But it is a vulnerable and brittle prosperity at the mercy of changes in taste and technology and liable to be threatened by larger and more efficient competitors and fluctuations in the market, which may cause not only economic hardships but also political unrest. Even Hong Kong, an exception in many ways to these pessimistic reflections, has had its boom restricted by drought and its industries hampered by a water shortage that is only just beginning to worry large western countries (see Appendix, p. 149).

In contrast to Hong Kong some of the most poorly endowed small territories have to resort to precarious expedients for a livelihood; gold coins are minted for Tonga in the hope that they will become collectors' pieces, curious shells and crustacea are exported to North America from the Turks and Caicos Islands, and new issues of postage stamps appear everywhere. Such exotica merely satisfy the whims of rich men and small boys: they are a fragile foundation for economic and political advancement. Some smaller territories see tourism as the panacea for their ills. It is no longer the preserve of the very rich and it can have a dramatic effect on a picturesque slum which can afford to sink some capital in amenities. It depends on rising standards of living in the affluent countries and surplus money for their inhabitants. It also needs improvements in the economic infra-structure of the smaller territory to entice those who expect accustomed comforts wherever they go. But expensive holidays in far-away places are one of the first and easiest sacrifices in a recession and one of the prices of political instability in a tourist resort is empty hotels. Only a small armed force is needed to effect a *coup d'état*.

In such ways the smaller territories seem weak and vulnerable and they make worse the problems faced by all developing countries. Normal hazards of life may be national emergencies; the task of their politicians is even more strenuous and exacting. But perhaps the gravest disadvantage of being small lies in the field of human relations. The process of forming a universalistic society, which has been going on in Europe for several centuries at least, and which some in the emergent countries wish to see completed in as many decades, comes up against peculiar snags in small territories with only a limited pool of manpower, particularly educated manpower. Here the conflict of small private loyalties with wider impersonal allegiances can touch murky depths among those who are, so to speak, constantly penned together for work and play. Private roles of kinship and obligation are entangled with public roles of office, and even if the elite be enlarged through educating the masses it will still probably be one in which everyone who counts knows everyone else intimately. Personal antagonisms can poison public affairs while disagreements over policy can estrange private life. There is little room for manoeuvre and, instead of parties based on intellectual convictions or class, factions may spring up which are only kept loosely together by various personal bonds. This is not to say that that this will inevitably happen but that it may happen given human nature as it is. Perhaps only a man of rare calibre can remain aloof and disinterested in an environment where it is difficult to escape into obscurity or to avoid meeting one's opponents all the time. After independence, when there is no longer any recourse to Whitehall and the overseas civil servants have departed, the political decisions are left squarely with those who have known each other since childhood.

For some the confined atmosphere of a small-scale society, which can also be found in larger states where the elite is still small, is distasteful, and herein lies another disadvantage of being small in the twentieth century. The larger countries offer a more bracing intellectual life and wider opportunities than the very small territories and the able are attracted to them. Youths who are educated abroad, perhaps at the expense of their governments, discover on returning that the country that once was home now seems like a prison. In spite of the prestige of their qualifications they seek a career in voluntary exile in the metropolises of the world. No country, least of all a small one, can afford to lose an administrator, a chartered accountant or a potential prime minister.

One other factor needs a mention. Much was heard in the seminar of the 'diseconomies of scale' in a world where the race goes increasingly to the largest as well as the swiftest. These apply not only to industry and agriculture but to nationhood itself. Money and manpower are needed for the novel responsibilities of sovereignty, for defence forces, for diplomatic representation, and for what Bagehot called 'the nice and pretty events' to replace the outmoded symbolism of the Queen's Birthday Parade. Even modern stadia and halls for international sports and conferences are a help in welding a new nation together. All these expenses even on a modest scale eat up a greater proportion of the income of a small country than of a bigger one, but it is hard to condemn them as frivolities when a bewildering number of new states clamour for recognition and a share in international intercourse.

These are some of the problems, both particular and general, which have to be faced by the smaller territories. It is too early to see the political future of those which have or will achieve political independence either alone or in association with other states. This last diminutive generation of Commonwealth members may follow earlier patterns or evolve some kind of micro-independence which is quite novel. For the very small units, mere specks marooned on the map, it is hard to envisage any political advance beyond what they already possess—Bermuda or St Helena for instance. For others like Pitcairn or Montserrat, the drastic and unsentimental answer of outsiders could be total evacuation. But this did not work in Tristan da Cunha. Perhaps the young people of islands like these will gradually move out and in the course of time they will revert to solitude and be as unnecessary to mankind as they were before Europe discovered them.

3

SOME ECONOMIC PROBLEMS OF SMALL COUNTRIES

A. D. Knox

ECONOMIC CHARACTERISTICS OF SMALL COUNTRIES

When we talk of small countries we presumably have in mind those with small areas and small populations. We would expect such countries to have two main features in common. First, it is likely that their small area will contain less diverse resources than might be found in larger countries. Second, their domestic markets will be small. Admittedly the correlation between these two characteristics and small size is not perfect. No doubt there are examples of small countries with diverse resources and of large countries lacking such diversity. Moreover, it is certainly true that a small domestic market may be found in some countries with large physical area, and even in some where largeness of population is offset by the low level of income per head. But, broadly speaking, it would still seem to be true that small countries have small home markets and lack diverse resources.

This certainly tallies with the high degree of specialization we find in small countries. They generally concentrate what resources they have on a comparatively limited range of products and satisfy their other requirements through international trade. We thus find that small countries are more heavily dependent on foreign trade than are large countries. This may be seen in the following tables.

TABLE I. Size of nation and foreign trade: richer countries

(1) Group	(2) Average population (millions)	(3) Average income per head (US $)	(4) Average foreign trade per head (US $)	(5) (4) as % of (3)
1. First Five	69·0	653	142	21·8
2. Second Five	15·0	399	176	44·1
3. Third Five	10·2	429	252	58·8
4. Fourth Five	6·2	360	234	65·0
5. Fifth Five	3·9	579	306	52·9
6. Sixth Five	1·3	447	374	83·6

Source: S. Kuznets, 'Economic growth of small nations', in E. A. G. Robinson (ed.) *The Economic Consequences of the Size of Nations*, 1960.
Note: Thirty countries with higher income per head, 1949, arranged in decreasing order of population size.

36 SOME ECONOMIC PROBLEMS

TABLE II. Size of nation and foreign trade: poorer countries

(1) Group	(2) Average population (millions)	(3) Average income per head (US $)	(4) Average foreign trade per head (US $)	(5) (4) as % of (3)
1. First Five	214·2	52	19·6	37·7
2. Second Five	29·1	100	44·0	43·8
3. Third Five	16·4	59	27·2	46·1
4. Fourth Five	5·5	84	56·6	67·4
5. Fifth Five	2·7	68	41·4	61·1
6. Sixth Five	1·2	101	65·0	64·2

Source: *ibid.*

Note: Thirty countries with lower income per head, 1949, arranged in decreasing order of population size.

We find the same relationship in both tables: the ratio of foreign trade to national income rises as population size declines. The main difference between the two tables is that this relationship is not as regular and the range not as pronounced among the poorer countries as among the richer. Kuznets argues that this suggests that 'foreign trade by the less developed countries is subject to the more accidental influences of the availability of world-wide marketable resources' (Kuznets, 1960, p. 20).

Associated with this heavier reliance of smaller countries on foreign trade is the fact that the sources of their imports and the destinations of their exports are generally fewer than for large countries. The concentration is particularly noticeable for exports. The average small country sells in a much smaller number of foreign markets than does the average large country. Table III contains some data on this geographic concen-

TABLE III. Coefficients of geographic concentration of exports, by size and by income per head, 1954

Group	Developed countries	Underdeveloped countries	Total
Large countries	29·1	45·7	37·4
Small countries	37·9	58·7	44·9

Source: M. Michaely, 'Concentration of imports and exports: an international comparison', *Economic Journal* (December 1958).

Notes: (1) A small country is one with a population of less than 10 millions.

(2) A developed country is one with an income per head according to U.N. data for 1952–4 of more than U.S. $300.

(3) The coefficient of concentration used is the square root of the sums of the squares of the percentage share of n countries in the exports of a given country. Complete concentration in the sense that *all* exports go to one destination, gives an index of 100. Complete dispersion, if there are 100 countries to which exports go and if an equal share goes to each, gives an index of 10.

tration of exports. For both the developed and the underdeveloped countries, the exports of small countries show a greater geographic concentration. It has been suggested indeed that in some cases the degree of concentration may be so great that the small country is in an essentially satellitic position *vis-à-vis* the large country to which it sells the bulk of its produce. On the other hand, we should note that a summary table like Table III conceals other forces which may also be at work. One such force is geographic position. It appears that European countries have a much lower concentration of exports than countries elsewhere. The latter have a lesser diversity of markets close at hand and usually sell a higher proportion of their exports in a few markets than do their European counterparts.

If the general hypothesis is correct that small countries specialize more than large, we should expect to find a second type of concentration in their export trade: namely, a greater reliance on a small range of commodities. Some data on this are in Table IV. Among developed countries we find what we expect:

TABLE IV. Coefficients of commodity concentration of exports by size and by income per head, 1953.

Group	Developed countries	Underdeveloped countries	Total
Large countries	21·4	57·8	40·7
Small countries	39·1	46·2	41·5

Source: as for Table III.
Notes: (1) 'Small country' and 'developed country' defined as in notes to Table III.
(2) The coefficient of concentration is that used in Table III, *mutatis mutandis.*

but among underdeveloped the coefficient of concentration is higher for the bigger countries. This seemingly perverse relationship for the underdeveloped countries may occur because the degree of economic diversification is affected by the degree of development as well as by a country's size. Clearly the richer countries of the world are more diversified. Some of the largest underdeveloped countries are also the poorest. Thus among these underdeveloped countries we have conflicting forces: large size makes for diversified exports while economic backwardness makes for concentration.

To sum up, we find in comparisons of small and large countries that the former have
(a) a greater reliance on foreign trade;
(b) a greater concentration of their exports in a limited number of markets; and
(c) a lesser diversification in the range of commodities exported,

except in comparison with some of the more backward among the larger underdeveloped countries.

In short small countries are generally more specialized than are large countries.

SOME PROBLEMS OF SMALL COUNTRIES

The question to which we must now turn is whether the need to specialize confronts small countries with any problems. In a world of perfect markets there would be no problem. Small countries would be able to offset the limitations imposed by small domestic markets and a limited diversity of resources by means of specialization and international trade. Unfortunately markets are not perfect and, in consequence, the international division of labour stops short of the economic optimum.

The problem falls under two heads:

1. What kinds of market imperfections restrict the freedom of small countries to sell in foreign markets and to satisfy their requirements through imports?

2. To what extent do they incur higher costs because of this restriction? We may examine the first question under three main heads: transportation costs; restrictions on access to other markets as a result of tariffs, quotas and the like; and imperfect knowledge.

It is reasonable to assume that a small country cannot influence the prices of its exports or its imports,[1] and thus has to bear transport costs on both. It follows that it makes quite a difference to its real living standard whether it is close to its markets and suppliers or far from them—whether it is, say, in Europe like Switzerland or in the Indian Ocean like Mauritius. Moreover there are goods where transport costs are high in relation to delivered price. Bulky or perishable articles are examples. If the small country is to produce these it probably has to rely principally on its home market.[2] If it imports them, it will have to pay dearly for transport. Finally, there are services which are important in our total outlay and which for the most part are not transportable. They range from domestic service and laundering to the provision of transportation and, most important, government. If these can be supplied at comparable costs on a small as on a large scale then small countries are at no disadvantage vis-à-vis large countries. But if they cannot be so supplied then we have a significant problem. I return to this later.

The second problem a small country may face is that of being ex-

---

[1] It is possible to think of exceptions, but the assumption is true enough for present purposes.

[2] Unless there are foreign markets contiguous to it.

cluded from foreign markets. If that were to happen the small country would lose the benefit of specialization. But the actual problem of small countries is seldom, if ever, as clear as that. We have already noted their typically heavy reliance on foreign trade. Their problem is rather that they may not push their specialization as far as is economically advantageous for fear that tariff or other changes elsewhere may deprive them of part of their markets. It is possible that the producer in a large country who is able to sell the bulk of his produce in the home market is spared this uncertainty and can thus develop his activities more vigorously, secure in the knowledge that his market will not be arbitrarily curtailed. There can be no doubt that this contrast is a real one and that the producer in the small country has to face particular problems of uncertainty. But the contrast should not be overdone. Markets within a single country can be sharply altered by tax changes and other governmental action. Moreover, if small countries could sell in a wide range of markets, which for the most part they cannot, their producers would be spreading their risks while the producers of the large country, selling mostly at home, concentrate theirs.

There is a further aspect to this second problem. It has been argued that many underdeveloped countries face a serious problem since the rate of growth of demand for their traditional primary exports may now be insufficient to absorb their growing populations and other resources. So far as this is true they have to turn to other products and perhaps to manufactured goods. If their home markets are small they may have to develop an export market in order to be able to produce on an efficient scale. If they can obtain access to foreign markets, all is well. But they may face difficulties. By and large the kinds of manufactures for which underdeveloped countries can muster a reasonable amount of skill are the simpler kinds: textiles, simple toys, and the like. Professor Nurkse has argued that 'for these as a rule, total demand is not rapidly expanding so that existing producers must of necessity be injured and displaced if such exports are to increase considerably in volume' (Nurkse, 1959, p. 39). The consequence, he suggests, of this effort to break into stagnant or declining markets is that established producers will be harder hit than if markets were expanding rapidly and they will try all the more vigorously to obtain protection against the newcomers. It is very difficult to assess an argument of this sort, since it involves us in political prophecy. It may be said, however, that efforts in recent years to restrict markets for Hong Kong's textile exports suggest that Nurkse may be right. If he is, then underdeveloped countries trying to develop new manufacturing industries may have to rely substantially on their own home markets.

We may now turn to the third type of market imperfection which may make the size of a country's home market significant for its economic development. This is the problem of imperfect knowledge. It bears on our subject in two ways. Firstly, it affects the ease with which new producers can win acceptance for their goods. Secondly, it has the effect that in many cases investment decisions are heavily influenced by the nature and extent of local markets.

The first of these suggests that it may be a good deal easier for a new producer to sell some products in foreign markets than for him to sell others. For example, a considerable number of primary products are fairly standardized and lend themselves to grading. In addition many are sold to other producers for further processing and thus to expert, informed buyers. On the other hand, many manufactured goods are branded and differentiated. Thus one would expect that it would be easier for a new producer to break into world markets for, say, cocoa or tobacco, than into that for some manufactured good. It follows that small countries may have to rely more heavily on their home markets if they produce manufactured goods than if they are purely primary producers.

The argument for the second impact of imperfect knowledge rests on the simple proposition that investors are influenced mainly by the market they know well and this is generally the market of their own country. The range of potential investments is thus likely to be greater where the home market is large than where it is small. There are, of course, exceptions. In some cases the knowledge of investors does not extend to even the whole of the home market. In other cases they appear to have been influenced by prospects in foreign markets. But it is interesting to note in how many instances this has been the consequence of the activity of foreign traders in seeking new sources of supply. In other instances reliance on foreign markets has developed where investors with particular interests and knowledge have sought wider markets in which to deploy their particular skills. But where foreign buyers are not seeking new sources and where investors have no special skill to exploit the characteristics of the home market are likely to be an important guide.

All the arguments we have reviewed so far are concerned with the conditions which make for reliance on the domestic market or on domestic sources of supply. But, as has been suggested from time to time, there is a further problem: namely whether the size of that market or of the resources matters. This is an issue about which remarkably little is known. We are no doubt safe in assuming that there are some economies of scale. As the production of a good or service expands unit costs of production fall until some particular scale of output is reached. Beyond this, they are constant or they rise. But that still leaves us

ignorant on two points which are vital if we are to assess the consequences of the size of an economy:
  (a) at what scale of output is least cost production reached; and
  (b) what is the pattern of decline of unit costs as the scale of production rises towards this optimum?
  The second question is important because it makes a big difference to a
producer operating at a sub-optimal scale whether his unit costs are only
slightly above those of an optimal-scale producer or greatly above them.
It is unfortunately a question to which remarkably little attention has
been paid.
  There are a number of industries where large-scale production seems
to be required for efficient output. Aircraft, motor-cars, heavy engineering, are among the ones that come to mind. But that still leaves a wide
range of economic activities. Indeed, it would seem to leave a sufficient
number to keep the total resources of most countries fully occupied.
Thus what we really want to know is, firstly, can those things, mainly
services, which a country has to provide for itself be supplied just as
well on a small scale as a large; and secondly, to what extent is a small
country restricted in the choice of commodities it can produce by
the fact that it may have to rely principally on its own domestic
market.
  For most services and for many market-oriented goods the answers
seem to be fairly straightforward. These are typically items in contact
with consumers and typically supplied on a small scale. I refer here to
such services as laundries, domestic service, professional and educational
services of many kinds, and also to such industries as baking, aerated
waters, building, and many others. There are, of course, others that have
to be supplied on a fairly large scale. Roads, railways, ports, and air-
ports fall into this category. To be reasonably efficient they have to be
fairly large.[1] Moreover, even for those goods and services normally
supplied on a small scale, it is difficult to escape the suspicion that small
countries may lose in some ways. One point on this has been put very
well by Kuznets (1960, p. 25). For professional and educational services,
'whose quality is dependent upon participation in the intellectual life of
a wide community, too close a tie to the distinctive language and the
limited professional group of a small country is a serious drawback. All
other conditions being equal, a country with a larger population can at
a lesser cost develop the variety of specialities in the intellectual hierarchy, and provide the tools for adequate participation in the world
community of advanced knowledge.' A further point is that some
goods and services are provided on both a small-scale and a large-scale
basis. The small country can manage the former but not the latter and

[1] Cf. Downie, 1959, on the airport problem in British Honduras.

thus it loses the particular services provided by large-scale organization. 'In the larger countries there is room for giant construction companies which can use more advanced technology in the construction of many large-scale plants, office buildings or apartment houses. There is room for well-organized chain systems of retail stores, repair service establishments and the like. And there is room for economy of scale even in local transportation, financial establishments, business services, and so forth.'[1]

Earlier I noted that an important service was government. Presumably there are some economies of scale here too. Certainly there are countries such as some of the West Indies and British Honduras, which cannot pay for even the government services they now have. Moreover it is likely, to say the least, that they have a standard of government service lower than that prevailing elsewhere. But we have no way of measuring the costs falling on these small communities because of this. Indeed here we have the nub of the problem of assessing economies of scale in government. We have data on public expenditure in countries large and small; but we have no statistics measuring the costs per head that would have to be incurred by countries of different sizes in order to provide comparable services. The only relevant data I have seen are some figures for Australia where, in connection with federal grants to the states, annual calculations are made of the costs of providing certain services. It has been estimated for 1955–6 that (Prest, 1960) the actual average cost of providing education, health, and law and order in the three largest states[2] was 357s. 11d. per head. The cost of providing the same standard of services was estimated to be 379s. 5d. per head in South Australia and 400s. 11d. per head in Western Australia and Tasmania.[3] These figures are illustrative only; but they do give some indication of the additional burden falling on small countries. It will be noted that they do not cover defence expenditure, which is a federal matter in Australia. Many have argued that defence is a particularly heavy burden on small states[4] and thus the costs of small size may be greater than is suggested by the Australian data. It is, however, a moot point

---

[1] Kuznets (1960), p. 25. See also Downie's comments on the absence in British Honduras of any sizeable construction organization other than the P.W.D.

[2] New South Wales—Population 3,524,379
   Victoria   „   2,564,849
   Queensland   „   1,352,629

[3] South Australia—Population 834,465
   Western Australia   „   559,040
   Tasmania   „   319,192

[4] Cf. E. A. G. Robinson, 'The size of the nation and the cost of administration' in Robinson, *op. cit.* Unfortunately the statistics in this paper tell us little about the problems of size.

whether this burden is as significant in the contemporary scene as it once may have been.

This still leaves us with the wide range of activities where a country may have to rely in part on its domestic market because of the uncertainties of international trade and the other factors discussed. Again we are hampered by the absence of data. In addition we have to keep in mind that the fact that a country may be unable to produce all of this group of products is no evidence of hardship. A country needs a government, transportation services, and the like; but it can flourish without steel mills, cement factories, and a great number of other types of production.

It is difficult to say a great deal in general terms. So much depends on the circumstances and characteristics of particular countries. But something of the nature of the problem may be illustrated by some data for American industries (Bain, 1956) and for output and markets in Trinidad (Trinidad and Tobago, 1956). This is a shaky exercise and open to all manner of criticisms; but it may help at least a little. It is possible to compare the minimum optimal scale[1] of five industries in the U.S.A. (footwear, canned fruit products, cement, cigarettes, and soap) with the output of corresponding industries in Trinidad and to some extent with the Trinidad domestic market. A straight comparison shows that for all five the U.S. minimum optimal scale is greater than Trinidad output; and indeed it is greater than the Trinidad home 'market'. This is the kind of comparison that is usually seized upon as showing that small countries like Trinidad[2] are at a serious disadvantage even with some of those commodities they actually succeed in producing. The further implication is drawn that there must be many other commodities they simply cannot produce because the minimum optimal scale is too large. If, however, we look a bit closer we find a somewhat more favourable picture. Bain was able to gather some data on production costs at sub-optimum outputs. Admittedly these are scrappy but it is interesting to look at them. For cement, costs appear to rise sharply as the scale of production falls below the minimum optimal level. They are 15 per cent up at one-half optimum[3] which would appear to be about the size of the Trinidad market. Thus Trinidad production for the home market, assuming a monopoly of that market, is at a cost disadvantage but perhaps not disastrously so. For soap, the sub-optimum plant is

---

[1] I.e. the minimum scale of output at which least cost production is possible.

[2] In 1959 Trinidad had a population of some 800,000; a gross domestic product at market prices of £171·7 millions; and a gross domestic product per head of about £214.

[3] Bain's data on the behaviour of sub-optimum costs are all in terms of unit cost at some percentage of the minimum optimal scale.

apparently at no great disadvantage. Costs are 5 per cent up at one-fifth optimum and 15 per cent at one-twentieth. This hardly suggests any great advantage to the larger plant; but we should note that even one-twentieth of the U.S. optimum is approximately twice Trinidad output. Cigarettes, canned fruits, and shoes show even less advantage to the large producer. Cigarette costs are 2 per cent up at one-fifth of the optimum and rather more than 2 per cent up at one-twentieth of the optimum, which is less than Trinidad output. In the remaining two industries production costs appear hardly to rise at all back to the smallest plant size considered; but even this size is greater than Trinidad output.

Let me repeat that these calculations are shaky and tentative. The point is simply that they suggest that a full investigation might reveal a wide number of industries in which the small country is at no significant disadvantage even where it may have to rely largely on its domestic market. The common type of comparison is inadequate because it contrasts simply minimum optimal scale in, say, the U.S.A. or the U.K. with the potential home market of smaller countries.

A CONCLUDING REMARK

For the most part the broad conclusion emerging from this discussion of the economic problems of small countries has been that they are likely to suffer a number of disabilities. But there is one highly important way in which they may have the edge on their larger fellows. It is a commonplace that economic development requires at times a good deal of social change. It requires the acceptance by a people at large of the need for adjustment. It may well be that small countries have a greater social cohesiveness to help them in this task. One can readily think of exceptions; but the basic point is that small countries may not have to cope with the same difficulties as large states in welding their peoples into one.

But this is trespassing on the ground of the fourth paper in our series. Suffice it to say that if small countries can manage change more easily they have a powerful advantage. If they cannot, their problems are great. No doubt the answer is that some can and others cannot.

4

SOCIOLOGICAL ASPECTS OF SMALLNESS[1]

Burton Benedict

'SMALL' is obviously a relative term. When applied to territories it usually refers to either area or population or both. In general I shall take it to mean both territory and population, but it is clear that more precision is required. In discussing the sociological aspects of smallness I shall be discussing roles, institutions, groupings, and values, phenomena more complex than square miles and number of heads, for they vary not only in size but also in complexity. What I want to do is to examine the social characteristics of small territories. What are the social concomitants of smallness? Are the differences between larger and smaller territories merely quantitative or are there qualitative differences? Do the social concomitants of smallness foster or inhibit development or are they of no material significance?

A distinction must be drawn between a small-scale society and a small territory. It is possible to have a small-scale society in a very large territory (e.g. the Eskimo or the Bedouin). It is also possible to have part of a large-scale society in a small territory (e.g. Luxembourg or Monaco). The criteria of size for territories are area and population; the criteria of scale for a society are the number and quality of role relationships.

Sociologists and social anthropologists have treated 'smallness' in two contexts. Firstly they have studied the small group as found within the society. This has been usually termed the 'primary group' or the 'face-to-face' group. Sometimes it has been the general characteristics of such groups which have been the focus of interest (e.g. Homans, 1951); sometimes it has been the study of particular types of groups such as the family or the gang (e.g. Whyte, 1943) or some other form of association. Such face-to-face groups exist in all societies and are not a particular characteristic of the smaller territories. They will not be my concern in this paper except insofar as they illuminate aspects of scale in a somewhat wider field.

The second main context of smallness has been the particular concern of anthropologists. This has been the study of 'small scale' societies.

[1] A slightly different version of this paper was presented at a conference on 'New Approaches in Social Anthropology' at Cambridge in June 1963 and has been published in Banton, 1966.

Indeed smallness in scale has often been cited as a defining characteristic of 'primitive' (e.g. Evans-Pritchard, 1951, p. 8). One should distinguish between two major types of small-scale societies. Both are composed chiefly of primary groups, but in one the total social field is small and in the other it is composed of a series of interlocking small groups which extend through a considerable population. Island societies such as Tikopia or Dobu are examples of the former type. The latter are exemplified by the segmentary societies (e.g. Nuer, Tiv, Tallensi). Nadel has constructed the model for this type of society:

Think, for example, of a tribe divided into a number of sub-tribes or extended families; these all duplicate each other, both in their structure and in their modes of action; each is relatively self-contained, and such relations as obtain between them (inter-marriage, economic co-operation, and so forth) do not follow from their constitution (their 'statutes'), but are contingent upon circumstances and outside interests. Though such segments may in fact 'combine' to form the society at large, they could exist without each other and in any number; one could add to or subtract from it without affecting the working either of each segment or of the embracing group. (Nadel, 1951, p. 178.)[1]

Thus it is that, for example, the Tiv of Nigeria who number perhaps a million can still be described as a small-scale society.[2]

One other type of small group frequently studied by anthropologists and sociologists must be mentioned. This is the village community. Redfield has stressed distinctiveness both from the observer's and the inhabitant's point of view, smallness, homogeneity, and 'all providing self-sufficiency' as characteristics of the small community (Redfield, 1955, p. 4). Yet it is obvious that a village community is only what Kroeber (1948, p. 284) called a 'part-society'. It is less self-sufficient than either the island society or the segmentary society, though, of course, there are considerable variations in this respect.

Most of the smaller territories which were considered in the Seminar are larger than island societies like Tikopia and more complex than the segmentary societies and village communities. Nevertheless they share or possess in some degree some of the characteristics of such small

---

[1] Societies of this type are held together by what Durkheim called 'mechanical solidarity', that is, the parts of the society act together only insofar as they have no actions of their own. (1947, p. 130.)

[2] The question arises as to whether such peoples as the Tiv are a 'society' at all. This depends on the criteria we use to define society. There are a large number of possibilities such as common language, descent, origin, religion, political allegiance, etc. Most anthropologists would take the criterion of the widest effective political group as crucial, i.e. the widest group which could employ force against outsiders and which effectively prevents or limits the use of force within the group. (v. Nadel, 1951, pp. 183–8; Mair, 1962, esp. Part I; Schapera, 1956, Ch. 1.)

groups. Chief among these is that their total social field is relatively small.

SCALE AND ROLES

The number of roles to be played in any society is to some extent dependent on its size, but size alone in terms of population does not mean that there are large numbers of roles in the society as the examples of the populous segmentary societies demonstrate. There must also be what Durkheim termed a condensation of society, multiplying social relations among more individuals and leading to a greater division of labour (Durkheim, 1947, p. 260). While this need not take place in a large population with a simple economy (as in the segmentary societies), it is more difficult for it to occur in a very small-scale society. G. and M. Wilson in discussing criteria of scale state: 'A Bushman, we maintain, is as dependent on his fellows as an Englishman, but the Englishman depends upon many more people than does the Bushman' (1945, p. 25). Yet it is obvious that there is a difference in quality in the dependence of the Bushman and of the Englishman on his fellows. The Wilsons describe this as a difference of intensity of relations, the intensity of the Englishman's relations being 'more spread out'.[1] I believe we can carry the analysis further than this, by looking more closely at the nature of the roles themselves. Not only are there fewer roles in a small-scale society but because of the smallness of the total social field many roles are played by relatively few individuals. It is a commonplace in anthropological studies of small communities that economic, political, religious, and kinship systems are very often coincident or nearly so. The same individuals are brought into contact over and over again in various activities. 'Different types of primary groups tend to coincide or overlap in large measure' (Firth, 1951, p. 47). Relationships are what Gluckman calls 'multiplex' in that 'nearly every social relationship serves many interests' (1955, pp. 18–19). This has important implications for economic and social development for it means that decisions and choices of individuals are influenced by their relations in many contexts with other individuals. It becomes difficult to remove an inefficient

[1] The word, 'intensity' is by no means clear. The Wilsons imply that there is some total store of intensity which is invariable for all societies, but that it has various distributions in different societies. Thus as the range of interrelations increases, the intensity of relations with near neighbours, etc. decreases. (They also include intensity of relations with past generations in the form of ideas passed on, but I shall ignore this aspect.) This strikes me as very difficult to prove because we are not sure how intensity is to be measured. One could argue that the intensity of relations between spouses in London was greater (v. Bott, 1957) than in a society in which, like the bushmen, there was greater dependence on neighbours and kinsmen.

employee on grounds of inefficiency alone because he is attached to his employer by kinship and political ties. Impersonal standards of efficiency, performance, and integrity are modified by the myriad relationships connecting the individuals concerned.

Another way of looking at the role-characteristics of small-scale societies is by using the concepts of 'particularism' and 'universalism'.[1] 'Particularism' refers to the relationship of persons to each other in all their particularity or uniqueness. Kinship relations, especially close kinship relations, are of this type. An individual's father for example is marked off from every other male by virtue of his relationship to that individual. Relationships of this kind have several other characteristics; they are 'functionally diffuse', that is, they are not centred about one or a few specific functions such as buying a bottle of aspirins from the chemist, but are varied in their functions such as the relationship between husband and wife which may include a myriad of economic, social, procreative, productive, religious, and educative functions. Such roles are affectively charged. There are strong positive or negative attitudes between the persons involved in particularistic relationships. They also extend over a considerable time span. Such roles are usually ascriptive; typically one is born into them. The standards of judgement in the role depend on *who* the person *is* rather than what he does.

This model can be contrasted with a model stressing 'universalism', in which the relationship of individuals is based on more or less fixed standards and criteria. The incumbent of such a role treats all others with whom he comes in contact in this role-relationship in terms of universal categories. A shopkeeper should treat all his customers alike or a doctor all his patients. The roles are functionally specific. The attendant in a petrol station has the specific function of refuelling the motor-car. He may perform other specific functions, checking the oil, inflating the tyres, etc., but all of these are very definitely circumscribed, part of the definition of the role he is playing. If the oil is low, he must secure the driver's consent before putting in the required amount; the driver's role is just as specific. He must pay a specified amount which is calculated automatically for him on the petrol pump. He applies universalistic standards in comparing the products and service and prices of this particular petrol station with other petrol stations. He could change stations without hurting the attendant's feelings, and without feeling any pangs of guilt himself. The relationship, at least ideally in terms of

[1] These ideas stem from the work of Max Weber and have been developed by Talcott Parsons and his followers in *The Structure of Social Action*, 1937, *The Social System*, 1951, *Towards a General Theory of Action*, 1951. They are perhaps most clearly and simply set out in an early paper, 'The Professions and Social Structure' (reprinted 1949). For an example of their use see Eisenstadt, 1956.

a model, is affectively neutral. It also has a very limited time span, even though it may be repeated at intervals. The standards of judgment are based on criteria of achievement, *what* a person *does* rather than who he is. It is performance and efficiency not hereditary qualities which are relevant.

These are polar models and it is obvious that both sets of features are characteristic of most role-relationships which could be placed along a continuum. Role-relationships change over the course of time as the same individuals continue to interact in the same roles. Insofar as the driver gets to know the petrol station attendant and vice versa so that they know each other's names, enquire after each other's families, and so on, to that degree the relationship loses some of its universalistic quality and becomes partly particularistic. 'The more two people's total personalities are involved in the basis of their social relationship, the less it is possible for either of them to abstract from the particular person of the other in defining its content' (Parsons, 1949, p. 191).

This, it seems to me, is what occurs in a small-scale society. Where the total social field is small, relationships tend towards the particularistic pole. Who a man is matters very much more than what he does in the Seychelles. There are strong positive and negative attitudes in the role-relationships in the business and professional and governmental complexes based not mainly on role-performance as shop assistants, doctors, and clerks but on family and friendship connections. Occupational roles become diffuse when they have to be looked at in terms of kinship connections and influence in other spheres of activity. Only the outsider such as the overseas civil servant can preserve something of universalistic orientation and can separate his occupational from his non-occupational roles, but the longer he remains the less possible this becomes for him, for the general population is not playing it this way. He himself becomes involved in a series of highly particularistic relations either with other outsiders who form a small clique with limited contact with the local population or with the local population itself.

Does this matter? Might it not even be a good thing in that a community might have 'greater social cohesiveness' pushing it towards common goals as Mr Knox suggested at the end of his paper or as is often assumed by those interested in community development? Two points need to be made. The first is that a strong network of particularistic relationships does not mean social harmony. The affectivity of such roles can be negative as well as positive. The intense factionalism of small communities is a matter of repeated observation (e.g. Firth *et al.*, 1957). They are no more cohesive and harmonious than groups found in large-scale societies. The second point is more serious and may be put as a question: Are universalistic role-relationships essential for economic development? There seems to have been very little work on this, but it looks very much as though this may be the case. Large- or even medium-scale operations would seem to require functionally specific roles. If such enterprises are to be efficient and competitive they must be based on universalistic criteria of performance and achievement and not on an individual's hereditary relationships with other individuals in the enterprise. The affective component must be as neutral as possible or rational choices in terms of the efficiency of the enterprise become impossible. We are familiar with these problems even in large-scale societies, but in such societies there are always possibilities of bringing in outsiders. The social field is large enough to permit this. In small-scale societies there are no outsiders. They must be imported from another society. There remain many questions about type of economy and its relation to universalism–particularism pattern variables. Industrialization would appear to be most dependent on universalistic role-relationships; cottage industries, commerce and agriculture perhaps less so. The number of alternatives open to a population in the economic field would also seem to relate to these variables. Smaller territories with their economic specialization might therefore be at a disadvantage in developing universalistic criteria. On the other hand there is the possibility that candidates for particular occupational roles could be chosen particularistically and trained to perform efficiently. To some extent, for example, Franco-Mauritians have trained members of their own community to fill nearly all the higher level managerial and technical posts in the sugar industry which they control. Such a system of course limits opportunity and may be politically unacceptable as well as economically inefficient. Again isolation from markets may aggravate the inefficiencies of particularistic relationships when compared with countries like Luxembourg or Switzerland which are close to their markets and subject to the universalistic criteria which govern these markets. Unquestionably the factor of development enters. The underdeveloped countries, even the large ones, are socially characterized by particularistic role-relationships. Their small elites reach into all facets of social existence. It can only be predicted that they have a larger potential social field for developing universalistic role-relationships than the small isolated territories.

SCALE, VALUES AND ALTERNATIVES

Universalism and particularism may be called value orientations in that an actor playing a role based on universalistic criteria is using one set of values, e.g. whether a customer owes one money; whereas the same actor acting in a particularistic frame uses another set of values e.g. whether his brother-in-law needs the money he loaned him. I think

I have said enough to demonstrate this point and to show that a particularistic value orientation is apt to dominate in a small social field.

There is another sense in which the general values of a society may be related to its scale. Where kinship, economic, political, religious, and other systems tend to be coincident or nearly so there may be greater consistency of values than in a large-scale society where there may be different values for individuals acting in different situations or even for whole sets of individuals engaged in very different sorts of life. In a small-scale society anonymity is impossible. In a large-scale society particularly in an urban setting it is possible by moving, by changing jobs, names, styles of life. A Negro can pass for white in the United States if he has a light enough skin and gets out of the area in which he was brought up. He could not do so in a small West Indian island. As there are more kinds of jobs and ways of life in a large-scale society, so there are more alternatives for the individual. In a small-scale society choice is limited, alternatives are few, and the choice of an individual may have considerable effect throughout the social structure. This brings us again to the question of social cohesiveness. It is difficult to generalize for degrees of social cohesiveness will vary from society to society even when we are only dealing with smaller territories. A society like Mauritius with its different ethnic elements each with its own religion and style of life is less cohesive than the kingdom of Tonga. Yet both are rapidly affected by any major decision or change. A strike at the Ford plant in Dagenham has little immediate effect on most Englishmen; a strike at a sugar mill in Mauritius has very serious effects throughout the island, not only economically but politically. Not just a few but nearly everyone would be affected. Decisions in the economic, political, and legal fields have a pervasiveness in small-scale societies which they lack in societies of larger scale. This is again because people are connected to each other in so many different ways in a small-scale society.

SCALE AND MAGICO-RELIGIOUS PRACTICES

In small-scale societies, where alternatives are few and personal relationships are multiplex and highly charged affectively, people often blame failure on the evil intentions of others. Where these cannot be demonstrated by overt actions, they are sometimes thought to be the result of sorcery and witchcraft practised by one's enemies. A man in the Seychelles who loses his job will not consider that this may be a result of his lack of efficiency or that the work he is doing is no longer required. He rarely blames his employer. He is apt to think it is due to the machinations of some enemy who wants either his job, his wife, or

SOCIOLOGICAL ASPECTS OF SMALLNESS

is seeking revenge for some past injury. He will visit a fortune teller who, by asking a series of open-ended questions, will lead him to choose his enemy. The man then tries to protect himself or injure his enemy by magical means.

On another level the worship of local saints, deities, or ancestors is a characteristic of many small-scale societies. These again are felt to be intimately bound up with the personal relations of the community. Ancestors are an extension in time of the kin group and are most intimately concerned with its welfare. Neglect of ancestors can bring misfortune in a way analagous to neglect of living relatives. How much this sort of belief inhibits the development of universalistic role-relationships is not clear. The Wilsons state that such beliefs must decline with the growth of impersonal relations (p. 162).

SCALE AND JURAL RELATIONS

Maine's distinction between status and contract (1909, p. 174) and his famous dictum that progressive societies have moved from the former to the latter has relevance in any discussion of the sociological aspects of smallness. Status in Maine's sense is what we have been calling particularistic role-relationships. They depend chiefly on birth, on *who* a man is. A number of anthroplogists have pointed out (e.g. Bohannan, 1957) that procedure in native courts is often devoted to finding out who the litigants are in terms of their descent and affiliation rather than in finding out what occurred, for it is believed that an individual's behaviour cannot be judged apart from who he is. The important thing is to restore good social relationships among all parties concerned (including the judges), not to conform to an impersonal law. Because of the multiple connections between litigants, lawyers, and judges small countries often experience difficulties in applying impersonal law.

Contractual relations face similar difficulties. In a contractual relation involving the payment of money, the only relevant question is whether or not the money is owed. It does not matter whether the creditor needs the money or whether the debtor can afford to pay. If creditor and debtor are brothers or close friends questions of need and ability to pay may take precedence over the strict terms of the contract (*v*. Parsons, 1949, p. 190). Where one is doing business with one's relatives, friends, and neighbours it is difficult to apply impersonal standards. A shopkeeper with close personal ties with his clientele will find it very difficult to be an impersonal creditor and this may well lead him into bankruptcy. It is common in many small communities for the shopkeeper who is the principal manipulator of creditor-debtor relationships to be of a different ethnic or religious origin from his clients. He is thus not so closely connected to them by kinship and friendship and this enables

him to be a more impersonal creditor and hence a more successful
business man (Benedict, 1964, p. 344).

SCALE AND POLITICAL STRUCTURE

Apart from external political factors and the costs of administration
of small territories, there are sociological factors affecting the political
structure of small territories. First may be mentioned the ubiquitousness
of government. In a small territory one cannot progress very far up any
occupational or prestige ladder without running into government. This
is especially the case where there are programmes of economic development. Thus government is an active party to nearly every sizeable
enterprise, not only officially, but again because of the multi-stranded
networks connecting the members of a small-scale society to each other.
In many underdeveloped societies there are small elites marked off from
the rest of the population either by ethnic criteria or by class barriers.
They often have control of the wealth and technical skill (including
education) of the society. They usually have a large number of depen-
dants or clients attached to them and are very often able to control the
internal political machinery of the society. Large-scale societies probably
have a better potential for modifying this situation as educational and
economic opportunities increase. In small-scale societies the elite must
necessarily be small. Opportunities for upward mobility are limited and
more easily controlled by those in power—again because the social field
is smaller. Obviously the homogeneity or heterogeneity of a society is
important in this respect. Where factions form they are not apt to be
simply on the basis of political issues, but extend throughout the social
fabric. Where there are ethnic, religious, or linguistic differences, social
cleavages may become even wider and more irreconcilable (e.g. Fiji).
Whereas, in a large-scale society, political relationships are only partial
relationships, they are much more inclusive in a small-scale society.
Closely knit family organization, particularistic ties within the community, traditional bonds of clientage or servitude, colour bars, etc. all
militate against social mobility whether in the political or the economic
sphere (*v.* U.N., 1955, p. 21).

A word, perhaps, ought to be said about the form of government as
related to scale. A small governing elite is after all not a peculiarity of
small countries. Literal democracy in the sense that everyone has a
direct say in government can only exist in very small communities
where everyone can meet and discuss a problem until agreement is
reached (*v.* Mair, 1961, p. 2), but even in the smaller territories, unless
we are discussing some of the very smallest islands, this is impossible.
Representative government takes the place of democracy in its pure
form. Theoretically a small territory with an informed electorate should

operate a representative democracy very well. The Swiss, I believe, claim this distinction. But in small underdeveloped territories with particularistic criteria this may not work well. Indeed it may be difficult for an opposition to develop.

SCALE AND ECONOMIC DEVELOPMENT

'In an efficient industrial enterprise, the basic criteria for the recruitment of personnel and the assignment of tasks must be the ability to do the required work and a sense of responsibility in performance. The admission of exceptions may mean the difference between success and failure. Hence the particularist spirit which dominates segments of pre-industrial society, both in economic activities and in public life, and which tends to place personal loyalties and obligations to kin and friends above other considerations, while occasionally helpful in building up family businesses, may easily clash with the demands of industry. It may foster extreme practices of nepotism—such as putting relatives on the payroll even though they are incompetent or do not report for work—which may have a crippling effect on a small industrial undertaking and seriously reduce the efficiency of even the largest enterprise' (U.N., 1955, p. 20). If we accept this statement, does the scale of a society inhibit or render impossible industrialization? Are there societies which are too small for universalistic criteria to prevail? Just how small is too small? Unfortunately there does not seem to be any very clear cut answer to this, though I believe research could be designed which would give more precision to the problem than we have at present. One such question is: What is the effect of the scale of a society on the specialization of roles within it?

Firth has mentioned (1951, p. 47) that there is less room for specialization of roles in a small-scale society. This is particularly noticeable in occupational roles. Even should specialist techniques be acquired, there is simply not enough work for an individual to earn his living by his specialization alone. This has serious implications for economic development for it means that a small territory must either train and pay a specialist for performing only a very few services each year, or must import him at considerable expense and loss of time and at competitive prices when he is needed or that the specialist must be a jack of all trades with the possibility that he may be master of none.

Another question has been discussed above and concerns the relation of universalistic role-relationships to various sorts of economic enterprise. The lack of alternatives for people living in a small-scale society would seem to militate against the development of universalism. It is not merely size in terms of the area and population of a territory, but isolation which plays a large part in fostering particularistic role-relationships. As the Wilsons have pointed out (1945, p. 25) there is a sense in which the scale of a society increases the more it is in contact with other societies. Thus an increase in communications with the rest of the world might tend to foster the development of universalistic role-relationships and impersonal institutions which most small-scale societies so conspicuously lack. Another possibility is that some sorts of production may be able to thrive on a particularistic basis. The U.N. statement mentions family businesses. It is possible that certain agricultural enterprises, commercial firms or craft industries may achieve a measure of efficiency on a particularistic basis. As already pointed out the distinction between particularism and universalism is not a rigid one. Competition either locally or in world markets is a factor which can modify particularistic relationships in the direction of universalistic ones.

5

CASE STUDY: BRITISH HONDURAS

D. A. G. Waddell

THIS paper attempts to discuss such of the problems—demographic economic, sociological, and political—of British Honduras as may be directly related to the smallness of the territory.

DEMOGRAPHIC

British Honduras at present has something of an over-population problem. In view of the figures—area: 8,900 square miles, population: 90,000, density: 10 per square mile—this calls for some explanation. Part of the answer is that some half of the country is considered most suitable for forest reserve, and there is in addition a substantial area of rather inhospitable mountain and swamp. But the present cultivation covers only some 7 per cent of the land area, and there is a very much greater area, at present largely uninhabited, which it is believed could readily be brought under cultivation and could support a considerable population. The problem is that much of this area is not at present readily available for exploitation, and that much of the most obvious over-population is in the country's only urban centre, Belize, which accounts for over a third of the total population. It is not so much a question of absolute over- or under-population, but rather of the balance between population and exploitable resources. This balance has changed for the worse most noticeably since the end of World War II for three main reasons. The first is purely demographic. The birth rate has risen from 35 per 1000 to 41 per 1000; the death rate has fallen from 19 per 1000 to 11·5 per 1000; and the infant mortality rate has dropped from 190 per 1000 to 93 per 1000. As a result the average annual rate of increase of population, less than 1 per cent between the census of 1931 and 1946, rose to over 3 per cent between 1946 and the census of 1960.[1] It may be noted that there is every reason to believe that this trend will continue for some time. The death rate may fall further through expan-

---

[1] Population estimates and vital statistics are published annually in British Honduras, *Annual Report of the Registrar-General's Department*; for census figures, see *West Indian Census 1946*, Part E, Census of British Honduras, 9 April 1946 (Jamaica, 1948) and Jamaica, Department of Statistics, *West Indies Population Census 1960*; Jamaica Tabulation Centre, *Census of British Honduras, 7 April 1960*.

sion of the public health measures which have already achieved very substantial results, and there is no reason to expect any early appreciable reduction in the birth rate The second factor altering the balance has been a decline both in the supply of and the demand for the traditional forest products. To some extent this has been offset by increased agricultural production, but the effects have been most marked in Belize, which has traditionally supplied much of the seasonal labour force for forest work. The third factor has been the 'revolution of rising expectations'—again most noticeable in Belize, the point of contact with the outside world. In short, in the 1930s the forests of British Honduras supported, with some difficulty, a population of some 50,000, at a rather low standard of living. It is doubtful whether they could now do so. But that is an academic point, for there is now a population of 90,000 demanding ever-better standards. How is this problem to be solved?

An obvious demographic solution is emigration—to restore the balance between population and resources at a lower level. But a very substantial initial migration would be needed, and it would have to be a continuing process to take off the bulk of the natural increase. Most doors are now closed or closing, and in any case British Hondurans seem to be much more reluctant to move than West Indians. Further, as Mr Smith pointed out in his paper, emigration raises new problems by reducing the proportion which the working population bears to the total. An equally obvious solution is an internal redistribution of population so as to exploit more resources and arrive at a balance at the present level. With much unexploited land and unemployed population it might seem simple to bring the two into juxtaposition. But there are difficulties. The Belize population has no inclination to take to the land—small-scale experiments on these lines have failed. Moreover, the fact that much land is unexploited is due to its inaccessibility, the absence of necessary common services, and the large amounts of capital required to bring it into production.

There is a third and less obvious demographic solution, which was recommended by the Downie Report of 1959, and was adopted as official policy in 1960 (Downie, 1959; G. B., Cmnd. 984, 1960). This is to achieve a new balance at a higher level through immigration at a rate of some 7,000 a year, calculated, along with natural increase, to raise the total population to some 300,000 by 1975. The sort of influx that was envisaged was of agricultural immigrants, backed by sufficient capital, and settled in large concentrations. These, it was argued, might operate profitably where small-scale enterprises might be uneconomic, and could support the common services essential to the opening up of new areas. Their production would increase the country's resources and generate urban employment, and their presence would enable the social overheads, particularly the costs of administration, to be spread among many more people. These might seem substantial advantages. But it might be noted that if prevailing demographic trends persisted a new problem of more orthodox over-population might be created for a generation or two in the future. More immediate concern has been voiced over the social and political problems of absorbing an influx of this large order. Above all there remains the problem of where the immigrants are to come from, and who is to finance the heavy initial cost of transporting them and settling them on the land.

Thus, while there might seem to be more scope in thinly-populated British Honduras than in many other territories for solving the demographic problem by simple manipulation of population, little progress has been made in this direction. In common with other countries the solution is being sought more on economic lines, despite the experience in many parts of the world that even the greatest economic efforts can scarcely keep pace with population explosion, far less rising expectations.

ECONOMIC

British Honduras provides an excellent illustration of many of the characteristics of small territories outlined in Mr Knox's paper. It has not a great diversity of resources—in particular it lacks useful minerals —and until very recently it has concentrated heavily on forest products to the detriment of agriculture, and mahogany to the detriment of other forest products. Its domestic market is pitifully small. This, as Mr Knox has mentioned, and as the Downie Report expounds at some length, makes the costs of services such as government and transportation very heavy. It also means that there is little basis for local manufacture. Indeed it is only in food that there is much attempt to cater locally for the domestic market. Even here there are difficulties. There have been well-established preferences for imported foods, which the local producer finds it hard to break down. Moreover with such a small market a few producers can cause such a glut as to render their operations unprofitable. With operations on such a small scale, moreover, the costs of transport from the agricultural area to the urban market may be such as to make competition with the overseas producer impossible. Nevertheless, locally raised foodstuffs have been seen as a means of avoiding excessive dependence on imports (and thus an excessive level of exports to pay for them) and the government has had some success in raising production by guaranteed prices and markets in such commodities as maize, beans, and rice, and thus in reducing the import requirements. But to a very great extent British Honduras still depends, as it has depended in the past, on foreign trade, exporting her products and importing the necessities of life. British Honduras also shows Mr Knox's characteristic concentration of foreign trade to and from a limited number of markets, and a limited number of commodities exported. In the 1950s usually over 75 per cent of exports went to the three markets of the United Kingdom, the United States, and Jamaica, and over two-thirds of the imports came from the first two of these. Between 1946 and 1951 five commodities—chicle, citrus, pine lumber, mahogany lumber, and mahogany logs accounted for some 85 per cent of exports, and in 1959 the percentage was the same though sugar had replaced mahogany logs on the list of the five leading commodities. Moreover virtually all the sugar and citrus went to the U.K. market and virtually all the pine lumber to Jamaica and other West Indian islands.[1]

It seems clear that British Honduras suffers because of these consequences of its smallness. It has to pay the cost of transportation on imports, and, because of the small scale, few of these seem likely to be able to be replaced by local products. In particular the possibilities of local manufactures for the local markets would seem to be very slender. There may perhaps be, as Mr Knox shows, more hope for a country like Trinidad than has often been thought. But one may doubt whether investigation of sub-optimal costs gives grounds for optimism for British Honduras, with a population of little more than a tenth of that of Trinidad. It would appear that British Honduras must continue to rely largely on the export of primary products. British Honduras can have little or no influence on world markets. Moreover most of her present products are not in very active demand. Sugar—the most lucrative development of the 1950s—is dependent on international agreements and cannot be expanded indefinitely for that reason. Similarly, continued guarantees for citrus from Britain have been conditional on no expansion of acreage. The pine lumber industry was built up on the basis of the sterling area, Jamaica buying from British Honduras in preference to lower cost, but dollar, producers in North America. A change in Jamaica's trading pattern could have a serious effect on the industry. In the case of chicle, competition from Far Eastern suppliers and synthetic substitutes greatly curtailed the industry after the Second World War.

British Honduras thus has to try to develop more resources—to produce new products and find export markets for them, and to supply

[1] For a fuller discussion of the economy, see D. A. G. Waddell, *British Honduras: A Historical and Contemporary Survey* (London, 1961), Chapter II. See also annual reports of the British Honduras Agricultural, Forest and Labour departments, and the annual *Trade Report*.

more of her own needs, especially in foodstuffs, from her own production. Some progress has in fact been made on these lines in the last decade. Large amounts of money from Colonial Development and Welfare grants have been spent on building roads to open up new areas for agricultural or forest exploitation. But this is only a first step. Much further capital is required before substantial new production can be achieved. This has not been easy to obtain, in part because of political uncertainty, in part because of a series of costly failures of Colonial Development Corporation projects after the Second World War, and in part simply because of the ignorance of potential investors of the possibilities of British Honduras. For example, investigations have shown that there are areas where cocoa, a crop for which world demand has been brisk, can be successfully grown, and the government agricultural department has been trying to stimulate interest in it, but without very much success. Another good prospect for large areas of the country is livestock rearing.[1] A market exists in neighbouring Mexico for more meat than British Honduras has been producing, and it is thought probable that with proper processing facilities more distant markets could be successfully entered. But again little appears to have been done. Rather more successful have been attempts to raise more food for local consumption. Apart from the guaranteed price schemes mentioned the government instituted a pilot scheme for the mechanized production of rice, and sold the scheme, with room for expansion to a scale adequate to produce the balance of the colony's requirements, to an American investor; and two Mennonite communities, who migrated from Mexico in 1958, with adequate capital behind them, are already producing agricultural surpluses and have brought about a sensational fall in the price of eggs on the local market. In forestry, the major problem has been the decline in the reserves of the country's traditional staple product, mahogany, and particularly of trees suitable for export in the form of logs. Mahogany grows in dense forest among a host of other hardwoods. If markets could be found for some other types of hardwood, costs of extraction of all hardwoods could be cut. Even if other woods could be sold at a rate which would repay the cost of production, this would have the beneficial effect of thinning the forest and giving the valuable mahogany a better opportunity to regenerate and develop fully. But, although there has been some expansion of exports of cedar, world buyers have hitherto shown little interest in such varieties as mayflower, santamaria, nargusta, yemeri, banak, and ziricote. Another development which now appears to be well in hand is the processing of the stumps left after pine lumbering into a

[1] For this and other proposals, see Great Britain, Colonial Office, *Land in British Honduras, Report of the British Honduras Land Use Survey Team* (1959).

resinous substance from which products such as turpentine can be extracted. A plant has been built, which, when fully operational, is expected to produce a volume of exports which will rival in value those of sugar or mahogany. It is not, however, expected to employ a very large labour force. While such projects no doubt help the economy, it may well be wondered whether such piecemeal development can keep pace with the rising population. At the same time one may question whether really large-scale development can take place without substantial immigration. It is obviously hard in a small economy to keep labour demand and supply in equilibrium. Indeed British Honduras has always been characterized by seasonal migration of labour between different parts of the country. The Belize 'creole' has spent the dry season in the lumber forests; the Amerindian or *mestizo*, the wet season in the chicle forest; and more recently workers have moved to the Stann Creek Valley for the citrus harvest, and the Corozal district for the sugar crop.

It is possible that at least a partial solution, both to the labour problem and to the problem of markets, could be found by incorporating British Honduras into some larger economic unit. This, however, is as much a political and social question as an economic one. The economic arguments in favour of British Honduras joining the West Indies Federation, which were reasonable, even if not compelling, failed to obtain a hearing in the face of social and political objections. The same type of objections have circumscribed any consideration of integration with Central America, and limited it to the level of international economic co-operation (Waddell, 1961, pp. 118–38; Downie, 1959, pp. 12–14).

In general it may be concluded that the smallness of British Honduras has occasioned some of its economic problems and, perhaps more important, has made it extremely difficult to evolve solutions to these problems. The economic outlook for British Honduras as a separate entity gives little ground for optimism.

SOCIOLOGICAL

The problem of whether a small-scale society tends more towards cohesiveness, as Mr Knox thinks possible, or factionalism, as Dr Benedict fears likely, is of little relevance to British Honduras as a whole. For it can scarcely be described as a single society. The population of British Honduras is divided into a number of distinct communities. The most obvious line of demarcation between these is linguistic; but ethnic, occupational, and geographical factors are even more important. The largest community is the 'creole' which comprises some 60 per cent of the population. 'Creoles' are English-speaking or more commonly speak the Creole dialect, which is closely allied to that of Jamaica (Le Page, 1958, p. 55); ethnically they are predominantly negro, with a substantial number of mixed negro and European descent and a small number of locally-born whites. They predominate in all urban occupations, and provide the main labour force for the timber industry. A small number are farmers, but most 'creoles' despise agriculture as an inferior occupation. The city of Belize is essentially a 'creole' town, and is the permanent home of over half the 'creole' community. 'Creoles' are also found in a number of coastal and river settlements, scattered along the roads leading west and north from Belize, and, in the logging season, in the main forest areas. Social relationships within the 'creole' community have never been systematically studied, but it is clear that a class gradation exists, and that it is correlated with colour. While there appears to be no real social impediment to mobility, in most cases a white skin means high social position, the coloured element tend to predominate in non-manual occupations, and negroes are in the minority in the non-labouring classes, partly no doubt because of relative lack of educational opportunity. Virtually the entire membership of all the Protestant denominations are to be found in the 'creole' community. But a very large number of 'creoles', possibly even half, are Roman Catholics. Most of the upper classes (though by no means all) appear to be Protestants, and, while many of the lower classes also are, there may be something of a religious element in class distinctions. The relatively privileged position of the lighter-skinned and largely Protestant upper classes is reinforced by the fact that it is with this element that expatriates (British, American, or West Indian), holding influential positions in government, business, or the social services, find their closest affinities. This is one reason why the 'creole' community appears to dominate the entire country to an even greater extent than its numerical pre-eminence would suggest.

Next in size and importance is the 'Spanish' community, accounting for between 20 and 25 per cent of the population. The Spanish language is the distinguishing characteristic of a group which comprises ethnically some Europeans, a great many *mestizos*, and a substantial number of Amerindians who have become assimilated. The 'Spanish' are descendants of immigrants from Mexico and Guatemala. They are concentrated in the north and west of the colony and predominate in the small towns of Corozal, Orange Walk, El Cayo, and Benque Viejo, and in a number of villages in their vicinities. Their pursuits are mainly agricultural—sugar in the north and cattle in the west. Some also engage in chicle production, and others in fishing. They are, with few exceptions, Roman Catholics. This concentrated, self-conscious minority is apparently not altogether satisfied with its subordination to the 'creole' element in the life of the colony, and there is a tendency for the 'Spanish' to think of themselves as Mexicans or Guatemalans, rather than as British Hondurans.

The Caribs, who make up some 8 per cent of the population, are ethnically predominantly negro. But their language and culture, which are more Amerindian, preserve their identity, which is also to some extent forced on them by social rejection by the 'creoles'. They are concentrated on the south coast of the country. Stann Creek is almost exclusively, and Punta Gorda largely, a Carib town. Most of the Caribs are engaged in subsistence farming (with cassava as their staple crop) and in fishing, but many work in the citrus plantations and factory near Stann Creek, and some in the forests. They also provide many of the rural school teachers. Most Caribs are Roman Catholics, but a few hundreds are Methodists (Taylor, 1951).

There are three separate communities of Amerindians, forming together some 10 per cent of the population. In the north around Corozal and Orange Walk, they have come from Yucatan. Here, their close proximity to the greatest 'Spanish' concentration has led to a good deal of assimilation and hispanicization. The same process has also taken place to some extent in the west, where a smaller number of Amerindians, Mopanero Mayas, have come from the Petén area of Guatemala. There is also one large Mopanero village in the south, but there the great bulk are Kekchi Mayas from the Vera Paz area of Guatemala. The virtual absence of a 'Spanish' element, and the remoteness of the area, leave the southern Mayas rather cut off from the other communities. Such contact as exists is provided largely by the Caribs. The three communities speak different Maya languages. All are at least nominally Roman Catholics, but often Maya gods are also worshipped. The basic way of life is subsistence farming of a very primitive variety, with maize as the staple. Some of the Mayas, however, engage in seasonal work in sugar, citrus, or chicle production (Thompson, 1930).

There are some hundreds of East Indians in the south, engaged in growing rice, and a similar number in the north near Corozal raising mainly fruit. A handful of Syrians are in business in El Cayo, and in 1958 about a thousand German-speaking Mennonites, of European extraction, migrated from Northern Mexico to two remote points in the west and north of the colony to engage in agriculture. Their tradition of exclusiveness and political quietism make it unlikely that they will be integrated into any of the other communities.

These subdivisions mean that the small-scale society of British Honduras is divided into a number of even smaller communities, within which the particularistic relationships to which Dr Benedict draws attention are prevalent. Between members of different communities, however, relationships tend to be more universalistic. As the outsider is treated differently from the insider division tends to be perpetuated. If the communities were large enough for universalistic relationships to prevail, it would be reasonable to expect integration to be easier, as there would be less difference in treatment between insiders and outsiders. Even within the largest community, the 'creole', particularism is noticeable. For example, politics for most of the 1950s consisted of being either strongly for or strongly against Mr George Price. Perhaps the most striking example has been the hostility of the 'creole' community to immigration. The main objections to this have been social. It has been feared that outsiders in substantial numbers would not respect the British Honduran way of life; that they might be politically more sophisticated, and take over the country's political life; that they might be Protestants, and upset the present precarious balance in favour of the Roman Catholics; perhaps above all they would be 'pushing' and grasping—animated by more single-minded economic motivations —in other words that immigration would mean that the present particularistic outlook would have to be replaced by a more universalistic one. While it is possible, using universalistic criteria, to conclude that immigration might be good for British Honduras, British Hondurans ask not so much what can immigration contribute to the economy, but rather who will these people be, what will their relationships with the existing community be like. While it may be said that xenophobia is a product of isolation rather than of scale, and could be characteristic of an isolated community of any size, scale is also important, for it is the very smallness of British Honduras that ensures that even a relatively small migratory movement could have dramatic effects on the society.

Regarding Dr Benedict's other points, it is much more difficult to be definite on sociology than on economics, for there is very little detailed information. Many of his generalizations, however, appear to apply to British Honduras. For example, government does have a dominating influence, and, inasmuch as it is centred on Belize, it tends to be very much in the hands of the 'creole' community. But it is no longer dominated by the small white elite. The question of the difficulty of specialization of roles is one frequently encountered in British Honduras. In the agricultural services, for example, experts have often not had enough expert work to do, or their services have been required intermittently at different places, and they have had to spend a high proportion of their time travelling about the colony. In these circumstances it has been difficult to retain experts—but experts have been needed in a time of agricultural development and experiment. The same sort of problem has arisen in a different way with some of the very few highly trained British Hondurans. In a small society it is difficult to equate local talents with local vacancies. British Honduran graduates even in such scarce fields as science and economics have considered leaving the country because it could not offer them the sort of jobs that would enable them to use their skills fully. At the same time other posts remained unfilled or filled by expatriates. One of the ways in which the problem of smallness may be overcome, is, as Dr Benedict suggests, by increasing contacts with the outside world. This has been very much a political issue in British Honduras, and leads on to a consideration of the external political factors.

POLITICAL

Several of the possibilities outlined by Dr Wood for the political future of small territories have been considered for British Honduras. Immediately after the Second World War the Colonial Office suggested that British Honduras might form a part of the projected West Indian Federation. This proposal, however, received little support in British Honduras, and although the colony was represented at pre-federal conferences it never accepted even in principle the idea of joining the federation (Col. No. 218, 1948). There were several reasons for this. In the first place, British Honduras had little contact with the West Indies. Until the end of the 1940s most of its trade connections were with the United States. Moreover such connections as there had been with the West Indies, had not been liked by British Hondurans. In particular Jamaicans—the closest of the West Indians—were unpopular in Belize. When the nationalist movement started, a new objection was added— that federation was an imperialist device to perpetuate colonialism. Perhaps most important, as a result of the Evans Report (Cmd. 7533, 1948), federation and imperial policy became popularly linked with mass immigration—which, as we have seen, was felt to be socially objectionable. There was, however, something to be said for closer economic links, especially with Jamaica: but when Leigh Richardson, the leader of the People's United Party, began to explore these possibilities he was expelled from the party and the leadership was taken over by George Price—an implacable anti-federationist. In the next general election in 1957 Price made the issue federation and Richardson and all his followers lost their seats. The rejection of federation was emotional rather than rational; but in the end British Honduras lost nothing as the whole federal scheme collapsed. There seems no prospect of it being revived in the foreseeable future in any form into which British Honduras might be fitted.

Another possibility has stemmed from the irredentist claim of Guatemala. Its origin is complex,[1] but the claim itself as incorporated in the Guatemalan Constitution from 1945 is simply that British Honduras is part of Guatemala, illegally occupied by Britain.[2] Britain denied this claim, but the parties were unable to reach agreement on a form of arbitration. In the 1950s Guatemala appears to have turned to pursuing her claim by political rather than judicial means, and to have attempted to build up support in British Honduras itself. At first it was believed that this campaign was having some success, and it was alleged that the leaders of the PUP were in contact with Guatemala. Price in particular was accused by one of his former supporters of being committed to Guatemala, and in 1957 he was expelled from the Executive Council on the alleged grounds that he had entertained proposals from the Guatemalan Government for incorporation of British Honduras into Guatemala. There seems, however, to have been little support for any such proposal in British Honduras, and it would indeed have been a negation of the aims of the nationalist movement to move from dependence on London to dependence on Guatemala City. When Price made his intentions clear in 1958 they were more in the form of closer economic and cultural ties with Central America, and possible future political association as a sixth independent state within the framework of the Organization of Central American States. This was at variance with the Guatemalan claims of complete sovereignty over British Honduras, which were voiced with increased vociferousness in 1959, and in 1960 the PUP went on record as completely repudiating the Guatemalan claim and was joined in this by the other political parties.[3] There is little doubt that this is the view of the country as a whole, even among the Spanish-speaking element, many of whom have closer ties with Mexico than with Guatemala. In these circumstances the Guatemalan claim would appear to stand little chance of success. British

[1] On this see R. A. Humphreys, *The Diplomatic History of British Honduras 1638–1901* (London, 1961). The Guatemalan point of view is set out in J. L. Mendoza, *Britain and her Treaties on Belize* (Guatemala, 1947); and the Mexican in I. Fabela, *Belice: Defensa de los Derechos de México* (Mexico, 1944). Mexico considers its claim to part of British Honduras better than Guatemala's, but has indicated that it does not intend to press this against Britain or an independent British Honduras.

[2] The fullest statement of the Guatemalan case is in Guatemala, Ministry of Foreign Affairs, *White Book: Controversy between Guatemala and Great Britain relative to the Convention of 1859 on Territorial Matters, Belize Question* (Guatemala, 1938) along with two series of *Continuations of the White Book*. This case is questioned in L. M. Bloomfield, *The British Honduras-Guatemala Dispute* (Toronto, 1953).

[3] On events since World War II, see D. A. G. Waddell, 'Developments in the Belize Question 1946–1960', *American Journal of International Law* LV (1961).

Honduras may associate more closely with Central America in the future, but it seems most likely that this will be from a basis of independence.

Independence has in fact been the aim of the mass nationalist movement from its beginnings in 1950. From time to time there have been differences of opinion on whether this should be inside or outside the Commonwealth, but for the last few years both major parties have been committed to working for independence within the Commonwealth. In 1950 complete and separate independence for British Honduras was virtually unthinkable to British minds. To be independent a colony had to be 'viable'—by which apparently was meant of relatively large population, with diverse resources, and economically self-supporting. This was necessary to support the trappings of national sovereignty, such as defence and foreign representation. It is true that there were, even then, some very small independent countries, such as Luxembourg and Panama. But these were not seen as desirable models. Rather the concept of the nation, as embodied in the 1919 peace settlement, seems to have dominated at least metropolitan thinking. But in the last decade the criteria for independence have been considerably eroded. Jamaica and Trinidad, considered ten years ago as too small to be turned out into the world alone, are now full sovereign independent states. This has been possible because the old idea of the nation is no longer related in a meaningful way to the facts of political and economic power in the contemporary world. Independence, which in face of the realities of interdependence, now appears much more as a relative than an absolute status, no longer seems as impracticable for British Honduras as it did even a few years ago. The 'critical size' for independent states has diminished rapidly in the last decade. Economic self-sufficiency is no longer a requirement. Aid can continue after independence, and indeed may be available on a bigger scale. The only remaining stumbling-block is financial. British Honduras has been receiving grants-in-aid of local revenue from the British tax-payer, and such grants have normally implied a degree of political control, or at least supervision over how the money is spent. In the long run economic development and a rise in taxable capacity could wipe out the need for such grants. But in the even shorter term, it would not be surprising if some formula were arrived at to make titular independence compatible with continued receipts of such direct revenue subventions. Full independence, in legal status at least, seems to be the most probable political outcome for British Honduras.

6

THE GRAND DUCHY OF LUXEMBOURG[1]

K. C. Edwards

IN a study of small territories the case of the Grand Duchy of Luxembourg affords some highly distinctive features which, in their particular context, are both significant and instructive. The first and most obvious point of contrast between Luxembourg and the majority of small Commonwealth territories dealt with in this volume is one of physical environment. While the latter are largely tropical or subtropical in character, with predominantly non-white populations, the Grand Duchy is situated in temperate north-west Europe and its people are entirely European. Another and equally profound difference is that relating to political and economic status. Whereas the Commonwealth territories are, or have been until recently, colonial areas and are still largely undeveloped or only partially developed, the Grand Duchy is a highly developed and fully-organized sovereign state. Its economic significance moreover is entirely disproportionate to its size, for although it is barely 1000 square miles in extent (roughly equivalent to the English county of Derbyshire) and its population less than 330,000, it is one of the world's leading steel-producing countries—and it should be borne in mind that after food, steel is the most important commodity required to sustain present-day civilization.

The term 'small territory' is of course a relative one. While Luxembourg is ten times smaller in area than either Belgium or the Netherlands and its population several hundred times less, it nevertheless falls into a different category from that of the tiny mountain states of Europe

[1] *Selected References:*

Edwards, K. C., 1961: 'The Luxembourg Iron and Steel Industry', *Transactions of the Institute of British Geographers*.

Hemmer, C., 1948: *L'Economie du Grand Duché de Luxembourg*, Luxembourg.

Institut National de la Statistique et des Etudes Economiques, 1953: *Le Benelux, Memento économique*, Paris.

Muller, P. J., 1939: *Tatsachen aus der Geschichte des Luxemburger Landes*, Luxembourg.

Treinen, J., 1934: *L'Economie Luxembourgeoise sous le Régime de l'Union douanière Belgo-Luxembourgeoise*, Luxembourg.

Van der Mensbrugge, J., 1950: *Les Unions économiques: réalisations et perspectives*, Brussels.

The official *Annuaire Statistique* (volumes for 1955 and 1960) published in Luxembourg gives full statistics of population, production, transport, trade, finance, etc.

such as Andorra and Liechtenstein, for the difference in magnitude between Luxembourg and these is far greater than that between the Low Countries and the Grand Duchy. It may also be of interest to note that among the small territories of the Commonwealth, Zanzibar (with Pemba) before it ceased to be a Protectorate in 1963, with an area of 1,020 square miles and with 280,000 inhabitants, afforded a close parallel with Luxembourg in size.

The consequences of small size and the problems to which they give rise in any such country may be considered under two heads, according to whether they relate to external or internal circumstances. Those relating to external conditions are chiefly concerned with political and economic relations with other countries, while those relating to internal conditions affect the nature and character of society within the country. In the case of Luxembourg the external and internal aspects cannot be sharply distinguished, for as a result of its long history both external influences and indigenous forces have combined to produce the present-day character of the country and its position in the modern word.

EXTERNAL RELATIONS: THE QUEST FOR INDEPENDENCE

In considering external conditions, a brief review of Luxembourg's political history is necessary. As an organized unit its origin can be traced to one of the vassal territories which emerged amid the disintegration of Charlemagne's empire in the tenth century. Its founder was Siegfried Count of Ardenne who built a feudal stronghold on the site of the present Luxembourg City in A.D. 963 and gained control of the surrounding lands. After Siegfried's death the County (*compté*) of Luxembourg, as it came to be called, rose to importance through the marriage of his grand-daughter to a German prince who became the Emperor Henry II. In 1354 a later Emperor, Charles IV, himself Count of Luxembourg, advanced its status to that of a duchy. At this time the little country reached its maximum extent, some four times larger than it is today. Thereafter each successive stage towards nationhood and effective independence was marked, paradoxically, by a reduction of territory.

Following the end in 1383 of the House of Luxembourg, the great dynasty under which the duchy had attained considerable power and influence, a long period of foreign rule ensued, first under the Dukes of Burgundy (1443–1506), then under Spain (1506–1714), Austria (1714–1795), and France (1795–1815). During this period Luxembourg was the victim of the struggle for supremacy among the neighbouring powers and in 1659 suffered her first loss of territory, Thionville, Montmédy, and several smaller districts being ceded to France, without any compensating advantages being granted. In 1815 after the Napoleonic wars

Luxembourg regained a measure of autonomy as part of the new kingdom of the Netherlands and was raised to the status of a Grand Duchy, but only at the expense of a further sacrifice of territory, this time to Prussia on the east. Soon after the separation of Belgium from the Netherlands in 1831 Luxembourg was at last given formal independence. This was recognized by the Great Powers in the Treaty of London 1839 but the cost was the award to Belgium of the western and predominantly French-speaking half of the country, now the Belgian province of Luxembourg. Yet this was not the final stage in the quest for independence.

The Grand Duchy continued to be ruled by the King of the Netherlands who by inheritance was also Grand Duke. A separate but restricted constitution was granted in 1841 (revised and liberalized in 1848) but it was not until 1850 that William III of the Netherlands deputed his son Prince Henry to govern the small country and to set up his court in Luxembourg itself. Other problems remained, however, among them the anomalous position of the Luxembourg fortress, considered to be the strongest in Europe, which was garrisoned by Prussia. On this and related issues, a settlement was eventually reached by a second Treaty of London in 1867 by which the Great Powers agreed to the withdrawal of the Prussian garrison, the dismantling of the fortifications, and the recognition of Luxembourg's sovereignty together with a collective guarantee of her neutrality. This was the charter by which Luxembourg emerged as a fully independent state.

Throughout the previous centuries a continuous growth of patriotism, rooted in an ancient community sentiment, marked the feelings of the Luxembourg people. In the nineteenth century the increasing desire for political integrity, simply and modestly expressed as *Mir wolle bleive wat mir sin* (We wish to remain what we are), was reinforced by a vigorous democratic spirit. Thus the first truly national constitution, drawn up in 1868 and modelled closely on that of Belgium, provided for a fully representative government with the executive power held by the sovereign, at the same time safeguarding the rights and liberty of the individual. This constitution, which is substantially that in force today, accorded to the Luxembourg community an exemplary and enviable degree of freedom. But it must be remembered that this small country achieved its independent status only through the sanction of its larger neighbours.

Both in the quest for independence and afterwards two principles emerged, each at variance with the other, which were to determine Luxembourg's relations with other countries. The first was the right of nations, whatever their size, to conduct their own affairs; the second, based on the experience of centuries of struggle, is that small states, on the contrary, cannot exist in isolation however strong their will to do so. To Luxembourg the experience of the past fifty years alone has made this dilemma brutally clear. Her neutrality was violated in 1914 and again in 1940, the second occasion in particular bringing dire consequences. In 1940, however, the measures understandably taken to ensure the continuity of the state placed the Grand Duchy in a position of compromise regarding the terms of the Treaty of London. For on the day of the German invasion the government, accompanied by the Grand Ducal family, in accordance with a prepared plan, withdrew to France and thence to England, thus embracing the Allied cause and later contributing to the war effort. Five years later Luxembourg units participated in the campaign of liberation.

These actions marked a turning-point in Luxembourg's history for they brought an end to neutrality as a condition of sovereignty. In 1948 the new position was legally confirmed by an amendment of the constitution. 'Our country', declared M. Joseph Bech, the Foreign Minister, 'understands that it can no longer confine itself to isolation ... the events of 1940 have made us, whether we like it or not, very modest participants; we are no longer neutral spectators, but actors.' Today the Grand Duchy, apart from being a member of the United Nations, is a member of NATO and as such maintains a military force of one artillery battalion. The basis of sovereignty has thus been radically altered.

EXTERNAL RELATIONS: ECONOMIC DEPENDENCE

In the economic sphere, as in the political, the viability of small nations in the modern world poses difficult problems. This has long been recognized in Luxembourg. To avoid economic isolation the Grand Duchy entered the German Customs Union (*Zollverein*) when it was created in 1842, a step which brought undoubted benefits over the next seventy years, for it ensured continual economic development resulting in a steady improvement in the standard of living. Above all it made possible the growth of the iron and steel industry which became the basis of the country's present-day prosperity.

With the collapse of Germany in 1918 the government of the Grand Duchy renounced the *Zollverein* and as an alternative sought an economic union with France. Since this was unacceptable to the French, a similar approach was then made to Belgium. Eventually a single Belgo-Luxembourg customs unit was established, the agreement, which came into force in 1922, also providing for the use of Belgian currency in the Grand Duchy in addition to the local currency. For Luxembourg, having long enjoyed the benefit of trade protection under the *Zollverein*, the new arrangement meant a change towards a free trade policy but the attendant difficulties were soon surmounted. On the whole the union worked well and so far as Luxembourg was concerned, Belgium's widespread economic interests and the trading facilities afforded by the great port of Antwerp opened extensive markets to her products abroad, supplemented by an expanding internal market within the two countries. Being a landlocked state, unlike most of the Commonwealth territories (though not all have good port facilities), access to a major port is a leading consideration for Luxembourg. Antwerp, Rotterdam, and Dunkirk however are all within reasonable distance. The economic union itself of course was not invulnerable and its policy was subject to revision from time to time according to the world situation. During the period 1922–9 it strove to reduce tariffs to a minimum and to develop trade with as many countries as possible, a policy which helped Luxembourg to maintain the steel exports on which she so heavily depended. With the onset of the general depression in 1930 it became necessary to impose tariffs on some commodities and to increase them on others. Further measures, taken largely in defence of the internal market, consisted of trade agreements, notably that with the Scandinavian countries and the Netherlands (Oslo Convention 1930) and a commercial agreement with France in 1933.

The prospect of economic isolation caused concern among small countries even before the outbreak of the Second World War. Not only in Luxembourg and Belgium but in the Netherlands too, there was a growing feeling in support of closer collaboration. Thus the climate of opinion was already favourable for the exchange of views between the three refugee governments which took place in London during the war, of which the proposal for the Benelux Union was the outcome. For Luxembourg Benelux was a necessity, despite the almost intractable problems which it involved for the agricultural sector of her economy, and its realization by specific stages in 1948 and 1953 afforded a solution to the general problem as the union with Belgium had done thirty years earlier. Since 1960 as a member of the Benelux group Luxembourg has been one of the six countries forming the European Common Market, a position which she hopes will afford her even greater economic security. As an important steel-producing country Luxembourg became a member of the European Coal and Steel Community when it was set up in 1952, and the Grand Duchy, which is situated in the heart of industrial Western Europe, found immense satisfaction in the selection of its capital city as the seat of the High Authority, the Community's executive body. The choice is regarded by Luxembourgers as a symbol of their support for international co-operation. It is no less a symbol of their rightful self-interest.

The fact that both the Benelux Union and the Common Market were brought into operation without the forfeiture of sovereignty by any of the participants is of great importance to a small country like Luxembourg. For, as closer co-operation develops among the European states and leads towards some ultimate federal system, the Grand Duchy finds herself at least on an equal footing with her neighbours in this respect.

Before turning to some of the details of Luxembourg's economy, one further general point should be made. It is that political unity and economic development have both been favoured over a long period by the existence of a stable government. The party structure has changed relatively little and since the last war the two leading groups, the Christian Socialists and the Socialists, have maintained continuous control either singly or in coalition. The two smaller parties, the Democrats and Communists, have held only a few of the 52 seats in the Chamber of Deputies, though two or three Communists are consistently elected from the industrial district in the south. Political stability has provided the necessary confidence for attracting capital investment from outside and for maintaining Luxembourg's role as an important centre of international finance.

THE LUXEMBOURG ECONOMY

Between one-fifth and one-quarter of Luxembourg's population is engaged in agriculture and the country is virtually self-sufficient in basic food supplies (grain, meat, dairy produce, fruit, etc.) though sugar is not produced and is imported from Belgium. In the prevailing system of mixed farming, however, great emphasis is placed on live-stock raising especially for meat and dairy produce which provide exports, mainly to Belgium. Along the Moselle valley in the south-east vine-growing occupies most of the hill slopes, from which there is a considerable output of dry white wine. Yet, despite the traditional importance of agriculture, Luxembourg's prosperity depends over-whelmingly on her steel industry. Steel output, which now exceeds four million tons annually, accounts for 80 per cent by value of the total national production. The country has few other resources however and to maintain this position at least 90 per cent of the steel must be exported, for home requirements are inevitably small. Steel-making moreover employs well over half the total number of workers engaged in industry.

Clearly, other forms of production occupy a wholly subordinate position in the economy. General engineering chiefly serves the needs of the small internal market; the quarrying of stone and slates and the manufacture of leather, beer, and tobacco are still smaller activities, though a few new industries such as the making of tyres and chemicals, in comparatively large factories, have appeared in recent years. Another source of revenue which is steadily growing is the tourist trade, for the excellent roads, attractive scenery, and numerous historic sites, together with good hotel provision, appeal increasingly to visitors from other countries.

The steel industry is concentrated in a small district of a few square miles in the extreme south adjoining the border with France. Here the rich ore field of Lorraine extends for a short distance into Luxembourg territory, providing the basis for iron-smelting, which was first developed on a large scale in 1870, expanding rapidly after 1886 when steel production began. There are now five integrated steel plants, in addition to a unit producing electric steel located just north of the capital. The focus of the industry is Esch-sur-Alzette, the second largest town of the Grand Duchy with 28,000 inhabitants.

The industry itself is largely dependent on outside sources of raw material and this dependence is increasing. It has always relied on supplies of coke from Germany and in recent years from the Netherlands and Belgium as well. Also, as the better quality home ore becomes less plentiful, there is a growing need to use supplies from the French side of the frontier. Today the production of ore from the Luxembourg mines is well over six million tons annually. Of this amount one million tons are exported as crude ore, chiefly to Belgium, but to meet the needs of the steel works another six million tons must be imported including some 50,000 tons of high grade ore from Sweden. The same applies to labour, for the requirements cannot be met from Luxembourg alone. Of some 24,000 employed about 3,700 or 15 per cent are foreigners, mostly Italians and Belgians. In the past the proportion of foreign workers was considerably higher but the growth of mechanized techniques has resulted in smaller numbers being required. Many, though by no means all the 'imported' workers are to be found in the less-skilled sections of the labour force. Then of course in the shipment of exports, which consist mainly of semi-finished products (sheets, plates, bars, girders, etc.), the industry is dependent on favourable railway rates in the neighbouring countries.

These features of the industry however are not peculiar to Luxembourg. The British and German steel industries, like that in Poland among East European countries, are all heavily dependent on imported iron ore, while that of France relies heavily on imported coke. The viability of such an industry is not so much a question of the size of the country as of its relations with other countries. Luxembourg's geographical position provides a favourable location for steel production but from the standpoint of its competitive position the industry must continue to be technically efficient because wages are high, in fact the highest in the Coal and Steel Community.

The steel industry yields important by-products. Basic slag from the steel converters provides a valuable fertilizer which is used throughout the country and has done much to improve agricultural output in the poor lands of the Ardenne in the north. Much of the electricity consumed in the Grand Duchy is generated at comparatively low cost from waste gases at the steel works, and in general the whole community has benefited from the great wealth produced by the industry. Thus the obvious theoretical weakness in Luxembourg's economy, the overwhelming dependence upon a single form of production, has so far in practice been its undoubted strength. It is the main source of the country's prosperity, the high standard of living, and the high degree of material and cultural development.

Nevertheless concern is felt for the long-term future. Despite the introduction of a few new industries, the extent to which the economy can be diversified is problematic The availability of capital may not be an obstacle but there is certainly no surplus labour. Already of the 45,000 workers employed in industry some 13,000 or 28 per cent are foreigners. The Luxembourg population moreover is not growing at a rapid rate; it has increased comparatively slowly over the past century. In 1870 it was 204,000, by 1900 it was 236,000, and in 1935 (the last census prior to the war) 297,000. Today it is 327,000. In the past decade or so the rate of growth has accelerated somewhat, partly due to a rise in the birth-rate (from 14·0 per thousand population to 15·9 per thousand) and partly because of the influx of officials and their families attached to the international organizations set up in the capital. The population of Luxembourg city has grown from 62,000 in 1947 to over 75,000 today.

Emigration from the Grand Duchy, once considerable, is now on a small scale, though precise figures are not easy to obtain. A few thousand Luxembourgers are normally domiciled in France and Belgium, either temporarily employed or permanently following a career in those countries. A few leave each year to seek their fortune across the Atlantic. Thus the only source of further industrial labour is likely to be among those at present engaged in agriculture. As farming methods improve and holdings are converted into larger units, smaller numbers will be required. The drift from the land however has long been in progress and industry itself must now compete with the ever-growing demand for workers in the tertiary or service occupations. A further characteristic of the industrial sector in the Luxembourg economy is the absence of any tradition of female employment on a significant scale and this may partly explain the lack of textile manufacturing. Nowadays however it is customary for young unmarried women to obtain regular employment but they are mainly absorbed by the clerical, distributive, and other service trades.

SOCIAL COHESION

Although the rural areas are losing population to the towns, the strength of rural society has not been proportionately weakened and village life retains a substantial degree of social cohesion. In this the Church continues to play a leading part but the influence of secular institutions, such as a village band or a football club, is often considerable. Although many Luxembourgers commute daily to the capital city or to the steelworks in the south and young people increasingly seek their careers in town, most of them return to the country either for the weekend or at fairly frequent intervals. There are few who do not possess friends and relatives in the country. Family ties and an appreciation of the relaxed tempo of the village are still strong inducements to maintain contact with the countryside, which, in the age of the motor bus and private car, is everywhere within easy reach. While the strength of the family as the social unit remains generally unimpaired, the stresses of modern life are nevertheless reflected in the increasing frequency of divorce. In the decade 1900–10 there were only 10–20 divorces a year, whereas in the period 1950–60 there were well over 100 each year, the majority of them occurring in the industrial south.

The conservative outlook of the farming population, while inevitably producing a measure of parochialism, is offset by a continual awareness of events in the neighbouring countries and in the world at large, further stimulated by the agencies of radio and television. Such an awareness results in a ready acceptance by the community of all the various improvements in present-day living, including technical advances.

In so small a country local patriotism is readily identified with national sentiment. Property ownership is a source of pride and property rights are strongly safeguarded by law. In the towns the great majority of businesses and many of the industries, other than steel, are family concerns. Some 85 per cent of the farms are owner-occupied and, while it is true that many of the holdings are now too small for economic working, here and there the process of amalgamation into larger units is making headway.

Social cohesion in the Grand Duchy results from the interaction of several factors. Among these the strong resentment at outside interference is historically the most important, reinforced by the existence of a national language. Loyalty to the sovereign and regard for the monarchy as a symbol of national independence, very reminiscent of the United Kingdom, is another important element.

Unity is further strengthened by the Roman Catholic church (to which faith all but a negligible fraction of the population adhere), since the country is organized as a single diocese under a Bishop of Luxembourg, who by law must be of Luxembourg nationality. The high regard for democratic principles and free institutions, less steadfastly held by some other European countries, is a source of pride among Luxembourgers who have long enjoyed the rights of free association, freedom of speech, and a free press, together with the benefits of enlightened legislation governing conditions of labour, social welfare, and public health.

EDUCATION AND THE LANGUAGE PROBLEM

Undoubtedly one of the most powerful factors in promoting social cohesion is the state educational system. In producing a fully literate and well-informed community, education must be directed both to the preservation of national unity and to an appreciation and awareness of the larger world outside. Education must therefore serve national and international ends. In practice the one is especially the task of primary education and the other is perhaps more specifically a feature of the secondary stage. Whether in town or country all children, rich and poor, attend the same schools between the ages of six and fifteen, and for over a century the instruction in elementary subjects has been standardized. This common schooling, compulsory and free till the age of fifteen (though secondary education too is virtually free), has been highly effective in promoting a feeling of solidarity as well as a democratic outlook which is evident throughout public life. A few private schools exist but these are attended by barely 2 per cent of all the children and are chiefly for girls.

A parallel achievement of education in the Grand Duchy has been the handling of the language question. In the early years the children are taught in the medium of the mother tongue (Letzeburgesch), which remains the language in everyday use by all classes of society. Outside Luxembourg it is spoken only by a handful of people living close to the border, in districts which were once part of the Grand Duchy. Apart from these communities it is not understood by the Germans or the French. German and, later on, French are taught, the former having priority in view of its close affinity with the national dialect, while in the secondary schools either or both may be used as a medium of instruction, with English increasingly taught as a third foreign language. All Luxembourgers are bilingual and many are trilingual.

Letzeburgesch, German, and French are all official languages, though since the last war French has gained in preference over German. It is customarily used in the law courts, while in parliament (Chamber of Deputies) both the Luxembourg dialect and French are used, the latter especially for major speeches. The popular press on the other hand is mainly printed in German, largely because Letzeburgesch, not being fully systematized in syntax, is not easily written. For the same reason only a slight literature exists in the dialect, though the long satirical poem *De Rénert* (Reynard the Fox) by Michael Rodange, published in 1872, should be noted.

It must be stressed that the absence of minorities speaking a foreign language exclusively has saved Luxembourg from political dissensions based on linguistic groups such as other countries have experienced. On the other hand the distinction between the well-educated and the less well-educated is to some extent accentuated by the greater use of French made by the former, while so many of the latter have only an imperfect knowledge of it.

Although there are technical and commerical schools, Luxembourg has no university. It is doubtful if such a small community could maintain one, but the lack of one is probably an advantage rather than a defect. For students must attend universities in other countries, mainly choosing those of France, Belgium, and Western Germany, although in recent years quite a number have been attracted to the University of Zürich. In so doing they not only broaden their own experience but ensure that the benefits of an up-to-date training are brought to their own country. An exceptionally high standard of education is demanded of those entering the professions. This not only makes for a high degree of competence but, in such a small community where openings are obviously restricted, it serves to some extent to prevent a disproportionate number from competing for the same posts. Competition is nevertheless severe and not a few Luxembourgers follow their careers as doctors, lawyers, and engineers in other countries, a choice which is made easier by their proficiency in languages and because much of their training in any case is received in foreign universities.

Arising from the effectiveness of the educational system as well as from the prevailing economic prosperity is yet another factor making for solidarity within the Luxembourg community. This is the entire absence of an underprivileged class and the fact that there are no really poor people. Although great variations in income exist, the lowest wages are well above those of many other European countries and there are many forms of social security benefits.

CONCLUSION

Luxembourg thus presents a picture of a small fully-developed and highly prosperous sovereign state. It is at the same time a closely-knit community enjoying all the advantages of modern life unhindered by social dissensions or political unrest. It exhibits the full and complex organization of a state many times its size and in this respect is probably unique even among advanced societies. Its democratic foundations and its international outlook afford some parallel with Switzerland. Its economy, developed on an industrial basis, is however far less balanced than that of Switzerland, and largely for that reason the Grand Duchy is a strong advocate of the wider economic integration offered by the European Common Market. She is fully aware, in fact, that her own destiny rests on increasing international collaboration in Western Europe.

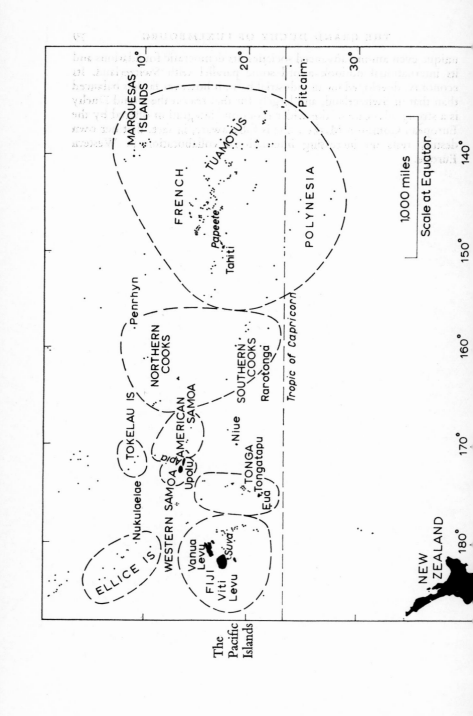

7

THE CONSEQUENCES OF SMALLNESS
IN POLYNESIA

R. G. Ward

WITHIN tropical Polynesia are found some of the world's smallest territorial units, measured by either area or population. The largest territory, Fiji,[1] has a population of under 500,000 while the smallest, Pitcairn Island, has less than 100 (Table I). Two territories, Tonga and Western Samoa, are independent states while the remainder exhibit a variety of ties with metropolitan powers. The territories considered in this paper are listed in Table I, together with their population, rate of population increase, and crude population density. But to accept the political division of the innumerable islands of Polynesia as a basis for analysis of the consequences of small size is unrealistic. Even today, when inter-island mobility is increasing rapidly, the real economic and social unit is often the individual island. The problem must therefore be considered at two levels, that of the political unit and that of the individual island. For example the Cooks include thirteen inhabited islands, scattered over 850,000 square miles of ocean, as distant from each other as London, Aberdeen, and Oslo. When inter-island shipping links are few, each of the remoter islands must form its own socio-economic unit for many activities. Furthermore, in this situation it is difficult to separate the consequences of smallness from those of isolation. Indeed the spatial isolation of Pitcairn and the Tokelaus is an important reason for their having remained separate territories, while the serious economic problems faced by many of the smaller islands would be greatly lessened were they close to some larger island or market.

In broad terms the consequence of smallness and isolation in Polynesia has been that the islands and territories have existed in an unusual state of vulnerability and instability. For at least 180 years outside events or influences, in themselves small and insignificant on a world scale, have had very severe consequences in the islands. Isolation has often precluded the introduction of new plants, crops, techniques, and ideas, but when that isolation has once been broken the small area and population

---

[1] Although only the eastern islands of Fiji are strictly Polynesian, the whole territory is included for the purpose of this paper. Hawaii and New Zealand are excluded.

of an island has given innovations a socio-economic impact much greater than would have been the case in larger territories. Chance, too, appears to have played a more important role in demographic, economic, and social change than would be expected in larger territories.

TABLE I

Territory	Population 1961	Average Annual Increase (rate per cent)	Density (per square mile, 1961)
Fiji	413,872	3·6 (1956–61)	58·8
Western Samoa	114,427	3·3 (1956–61)	100·9
American Samoa	20,051 (1960)	0·6 (1950–60)	263·8 (1960)
Tonga	56,838 (1956)	3·3 (1939–56)	211·3 (1956)
Cook Islands	18,378	2·0 (1956–61)	197·6
French Polynesia	73,201 (1956)	2·2 (1946–56)	48·8 (1956)
Niue	4,864	0·7 (1956–61)	c. 48
Tokelaus	1,860	2·8 (1956–61)	476·9
Pitcairn*	85 (1964)	−3·7 (1934–64)	c. 45 (1964)

* Figure derived from statement by Commissioner, South Pacific Office, Suva, reported in *Pacific Islands Monthly*, 35, March 1964, p. 13, and *Pacific Islands Monthly*, 32, July 1962, p. 66. All other figures are from official censuses or estimates.

THE HABITAT

The distinction between the atolls and other 'low' islands of coralline limestone, and the 'high' islands of volcanic, sedimentary, or metamorphic rocks, is of great importance in assessing habitability and economic potential. On the atolls and other limestone islands, soils are generally thin and sandy and the potential range of economic plants is very restricted. Throughout Polynesia isolation and distance from the main sources of plant dispersal have meant that the number of plant families represented is small (Zimmerman, 1963, pp. 58–9) and although the number of economic (and other) plants has greatly increased following European contact, the low islands have scarcely benefited at all. For them the only exception to the generally narrow resource range resulting from paucity of soil and economic plants is that of marine resources. And, though these are of critical importance in maintaining high population densities on many of these islands, they have been known to fail.

The nature of water supplies on the low islands adds to the vulnerability of their fragile resource base. As their elevation is rarely more than a few feet, their rainfall is not orographic, but the result of atmospheric instability. This and the location of many of the low islands within the tongue of low precipitation which extends across the central Pacific results in variability of rainfall much greater than on most larger and 'high' islands. For both drinking supplies and plant growth the freshwater lens in the subsoil and basement of reef rock is of vital importance. If, for example, the lens becomes saline either through prolonged drought, or from flooding by sea water resulting from typhoons or *tsunami*, the continued existence of the community may be threatened and food and export crops destroyed. Many atolls and small islands have, within living memory, suffered severely from hurricanes or near-hurricanes and from prolonged droughts.[1] In the past such damage has acted as an important curb to population growth though the possibility of external aid renders this less likely today. Nevertheless, the almost complete destruction of an island's entire export economy by natural forces is something which larger islands, even those the size of Viti Levu, Fiji, rarely if ever experience.

In addition to their greater capacity to absorb flood or storm damage, the larger islands are less vulnerable because of the wider range of ecological sites available. Furthermore they have benefited from the introduction of a relatively wide range of crops. Nevertheless they do share some risks with the small islands, such as that from crop diseases and pests which may spread throughout a wide area before counter-measures can be found. The smaller the island, however, the less the reserve of space or alternative crops to absorb the shock; hence the elaborate precautions to keep the rhinoceros beetle (*Oryctes rhinoceros* L.) out of French Polynesia, the seriousness of recent attacks on coconut palms by red beetles in Tikopia (*Pacific Islands Monthly*, July 1962, p. 159) and the concern over the spread of 'bunchy top' (a virus disease spread by the aphid *Pentalonia nigronervosa*) in Western Samoa banana groves.

None of the low or other limestone islands of Polynesia have any mineral resources other than phosphate and, in economic quantities, this has an extremely restricted occurrence. The larger islands lying to the west of the sial (or andesite) line (of which Viti Levu and Vanua Levu, Fiji, are within the area under study) have a variety of sedimentary, metamorphic, and volcanic rocks and a range of minerals of exploitable concentration and quantity. In Fiji gold has provided a stable third export by value for over twenty years and given rise to the Colony's third urban centre. It is evident, therefore, that relative size,

---

[1] For example, the hurricane of 18 January 1960 rendered 4,000 of Niue's 4,780 people homeless, left only 134 houses standing, and completely wiped out copra production for two years. This was the second hurricane within a year. For a graphic description of drought conditions see Grimble, A., 1957: *Return to the Islands*, London, pp. 34–9.

combined with location, has a considerable bearing on the economic potential of the Polynesian islands. The potential of the habitat becomes of increasing significance with the widening of economic dependence which accompanies economic development, and it appears that the narrow resource base and vulnerability of the smaller islands is becoming an increasing liability.

THE POPULATION

The small size of individual islands must, at any given level of technology and accepted standard of living, provide some limit to the size of population. When small size is combined with restricted habitat potential, and when isolation gives some protection from disease, the likelihood of overpopulation is increased. Taeuber has postulated that present demographic processes in most of the island ecosystems are inherently unstable and that growth is the pervasive process (1963, p. 227). It seems likely that this situation also existed in the pre-European era in Polynesia and there is evidence that overpopulation caused emigration from some small islands.

In addition to those stemming from potential and actual overpopulation, the small islands of Polynesia have always exhibited other features of demographic instability. Some arise from natural calamities but the small size of the populations themselves leaves them open to the risk of marked variations in both age and sex distributions through chance fluctuations in births and deaths. There are approximately 180 islands within Polynesia with a population of under 1,000 (of which about 140 have fewer than 500 people) and the age and sex structures of these smaller islands are typically irregular (Ward, 1961, pp. 6–8).

After the first European contacts with Polynesia, the population became more vulnerable and more liable to rapid fluctuation in size. New diseases devastated the population of many islands and even in the largest territory of Fiji between 20,000 and 30,000 people, perhaps one-sixth of the population, died directly or indirectly as a result of the 1875 measles epidemic.[1] Other violent fluctuations resulted from the activities of labour recruiters who, using persuasion or force, removed hundreds from certain islands. About 1,000 people, approximately half the population, were taken from Penrhyn Island (Northern Cooks) by these 'blackbirders' (G.B. *Pacific Islands*, 1943, p. 552) while 300 out of 400 were removed from the island of Nukulaelae (Ellice Group) soon after 1860 (G.B., *Pacific Islands*, 1944, p. 383). Voluntary emigration has had similar, though generally less severe results. In cases where

---

[1] Some estimates put the figure at 40,000 but McArthur suggests that this is too high. McArthur, N., n.d.: *The Population of the Pacific Islands*, Part 6, Canberra, pp. 263–5.

labourers were returned to their own or other islands they frequently carried new diseases and thus began another phase of depopulation.

During the present century the small size which laid the islands open to rapid depopulation has been one factor enabling a rapid reversal of the fall in numbers. New methods of child care and hygiene, and campaigns against a variety of diseases have quickly attained virtually blanket coverage and the change from a declining or stable to a rapidly increasing population has often been sudden. Unfortunately new social checks on population increase have not developed and birth rates remain high. For example the crude death rate in Western Samoa was 22 per thousand in 1922 but only 12 per thousand in 1932 (Lambert, 1934, p. 13). The population doubled in the next twenty-three years. Between 1956 and 1961 the death rate in the Cook Islands fell from 16·4 to 8·7 per thousand though the birth rate remained high at 49 per thousand (N.Z., 1957, p. 44; 1962, p. 41).

As indicated in Table I all territories, other than those with opportunities for emigration, are experiencing rapid population increase. Table II sets out the projected average annual rates of growth in total population and male work force of the major territories for 1961–6 and 1966–71 assuming no changes in age-specific death rates and no emigration.

TABLE II

Territory	Projected Average Annual Population Increase %		Projected Average Annual Increase in Male Work Force %	
	1961–6	1966–71	1961–6	1966–71
Fiji	3·58	3·60	3·60	3·45
Western Samoa	3·27	3·35	4·02	3·83
American Samoa	3·40	3·47	—	—
Tonga	3·26	3·26	3·22	3·45
Cook Islands	3·24	3·22	—	—
French Polynesia	3·28	3·20	2·35	3·18

Source: N. McArthur, 'Population and Social Change: Prospect for Polynesia', *Journ. Polynesian Society* **70**, 4, December 1961, pp. 396–7.

Natural increase rates of this order are amongst the highest in the world and the problems they create are accentuated by the fact that all the territories are primarily dependent upon agriculture and have strictly limited land areas. The crude density figures given in Table I seriously understate the position as they make no allowance for the considerable areas which are unusable. Few accurate statistics are available to show how much land is already used and how much more might be used but in Fiji 38 per cent of the total area is 'largely unsuited to permanent agriculture' and a further 32 per cent requires 'major improvements' before permanent agriculture can be safely practised (Wright and Twyford). In 1961 the density of population in relation to potential arable land which might be used without major improvements was over 500 persons per square mile. In Rarotonga, the largest of the Cook Islands, the density per square mile of land suitable for annual and tree crops was 1,170 in 1963 (Wright and Twyford; G.B. *Fiji Report*, 1962, p. 11; N.Z., 1964, pp. 10 and 18). Given densities of this order, it appears unlikely that the projected increases in the work forces can be supported by agriculture, particularly when farmers are turning increasingly to commercial production and requiring larger areas per family. In larger countries, or in those better endowed with other resources (or locations) this problem may be resolved by industrialization and urbanization. As is indicated below, small size and isolation render this less feasible in Polynesia.

Increased numbers press on small areas and limited resources quickly and directly. Borrie, Spillius, and Firth have suggested that in terms of local resources Tikopia is near the Malthusian limit of its population-carrying capacity (1957, p. 238) and similar situations have occurred elsewhere in the Pacific.

One possible solution is migration—both internal, to relieve local difficulties, and external to relieve problems on the larger, territory-wide scale. In almost every group people are moving from the smaller to the larger islands, from remote areas to districts near the towns and ports, from inaccessible to accessible areas and from rural to urban areas. But such movements are not always from overpopulated to underpopulated areas and it may be difficult to persuade people to change their preferred destinations and bring about what might appear more rational distributions. Attempts in Tonga, for example, to encourage people to move from increasingly crowded Tongatabu to the relatively thinly populated island of Eua have been unsuccessful. The main attractions for migrants are educational opportunities, non-agricultural employment (especially white-collar jobs) and the excitement of urban life. Vacant potential agricultural land is another attraction but is generally less powerful than the others. These incentives can rarely be provided on the smaller islands.

The very small islands (and the less accessible and more 'traditional' areas of the larger islands) provide many examples of particularistic societies (see Benedict, *supra*, pp. 48–50). Furthermore, except where located close to larger islands and forming part of a single economic unit, the total social field is very small. Occupational specialization is rare, and because of the limited size of the market for specialized services, is likely to remain so. Everyone is gardener, fisherman, housebuilder, and general labourer. While an island maintains a subsistence economy this, and the particularistic nature of society, raises few problems, but the increase in the commercial element in island economies has been accompanied by increasing universalism and by associated changes from communal to more individual forms of land tenure and labour organization (Sahlins, 1962; Ward, 1964, pp. 484–506). On the very small islands this may create particularly marked tensions as it is almost impossible for an individual to separate his various roles. Yet the desire to do so appears to be strengthening among many Polynesians and is an important factor encouraging migration to the large islands and the more universalistic societies of the towns of Suva, Papeete, Apia, or Avarua. Within the territories therefore, the contrast in habitat potential between the small and large islands is being reflected in and accentuated by migration, to the detriment of the small island communities.

Inhabitants of five territories, American Samoa, Cook Islands, Niue, Tokelaus, and Pitcairn, have had the opportunity of emigrating relatively freely to countries outside the region under study. The movement of American Samoans to Hawaii and mainland United States, and of Niueans and Cook Islanders to New Zealand, has greatly reduced the rate of population increase. In fact the population of American Samoa fell slightly between 1956 and 1960. But it is unlikely that any other territory will be able to solve its population problems in this manner and small land areas will continue to aggravate pressure of population until birth control reduces rates of increase.

THE ECONOMIC CONSEQUENCES OF SMALLNESS

The extent to which Polynesia's demographic problems, themselves partially a consequence of smallness, can be solved or ameliorated depends largely on the prospects for economic development. And these prospects, together with the present economic state, are greatly affected by the small size of islands and territories. The Polynesian territories exhibit many of the economic characteristics of small countries as described by Knox (*supra*, pp. 33–8). Their lack of a diverse physical resource base has been noted and all the territories are dependent upon a narrow range of exports and a restricted number of trade partners. Although there is little information available, it is clear that foreign trade accounts for a high proportion of national income in all territories.

The restricted range of exports, the small number of markets and the fact that many of the products have little elasticity of demand means that the territories are very susceptible to price fluctuations and have limited opportunities to counter unfavourable conditions.[1] The total

---

[1] For example, the Fiji price of copra has varied from £F4 to £F80 within the last thirty years.

TABLE III

	Percentage of total exports by value contributed by 1st and 2nd products 1960		Percentage of total imports/exports from or to leading trade partner 1960	
			Exports	Imports
Fiji	56 (sugar)	13 (copra)	45·6 (U.K.)	27·6 (Aust.)
American Samoa	96 (fish)	2 (copra)	99·6 (U.S.)	80·9 (U.S.)
Western Samoa	41 (copra)	29 (cocoa)	41·1 (N.Z.)	28·9 (N.Z.)
Tonga	81 (copra)	13 (bananas)	42·5 (U.K.)	25·0 (Aust.)
Cooks (1961)	43 (citrus, including fruit juice)	16 (apparel)	93·8 (N.Z.)	66·0 (N.Z.)
Niue (1961)	41 (kumaras)	15 (bananas)	82·6 (N.Z.)	70·7 (N.Z.)
French Polynesia	38 (phosphate)	34 (copra)	48·7 (Fr.)	47·5 (Fr.)

Sources: Official sources quoted in N.Z. Dept. of Industries and Commerce, *Pacific Islands—Handbook for Trade Mission*, Wellington, 1962. Dept. of Island Territories, *Report on Cook, Niue and Tokelau Islands*, Wellington, 1964, pp. 57–8, 92–3.

volume of produce from Polynesia as a whole is small compared with world export trade in the main commodities (e.g. 1960: Polynesia produced 3·8 per cent of the world's copra; 1·3 per cent of sugar; 0·8 per cent of bananas; 0·4 per cent of cocoa) (F.A.O., 1961) so that the territories can have little influence on world prices. This problem is accentuated by location far from major world markets compared to the West Indies, Ceylon, or West Africa. Only the limited markets of Australia and New Zealand are close at hand (and then at least 1,200 miles away) but the former protects her own tropical producers by import controls and duties. New Zealand is also an insecure market as imports, of bananas for example, have been restricted from time to time because of that country's own trade problems. Vulnerability is therefore a marked characteristic of Polynesian economies and one which it will be difficult to remove.

The smallest islands have the poorest economic prospects. Because of the restricted range of soils, there is little likelihood of the low islands being able to widen their range of export crops, even if there were adequate unused land. The smaller 'high' islands may have better prospects for growing new crops but frequently their small size and present high population density means that little additional cropland is available. Furthermore, their limited area restricts total output and means that the volume of produce which may be uplifted by a vessel on one call is small and often uneconomic unless visits are widely spaced. Crops which can be stored with little deterioration are the only possible sources of cash and, with increasing size of vessels, the number of visits per year has tended to decline. The chance of producing a range of cash crops has thus decreased. The greater the isolation, the greater the problem.

Throughout the Pacific stresses are arising with the change from a subsistence to a commercial economy and in the smaller islands this change may be the catalyst which raises socio-economic problems to a critical point and which accentuates population pressure. The production of a surplus for export frequently requires cultivation of a greater area per planter or per household than was formerly necessary for subsistence. Furthermore there is a tendency towards specialization in production of a narrow crop range and on the use of particular soil types. The change from bush fallowing to sedentary forms of agriculture, implicit in the adoption of many cash crops such as coconuts, cocoa, or coffee, has emphasized the value of the most fertile soils and reduced the relative value of poorer land. Further changes result from the increased demands on an individual's time, and labour is often devoted to cash crops at the expense of food gardens. The more laborious techniques tend to be abandoned and labour-demanding crops (e.g. yams) may be replaced by less demanding crops such as tapioca or by dependence on imported food. Such changes may result in a reduction of the area which the islanders consider to be usable. For example, with the virtual abandonment of irrigated taro cultivation on terraced slopes and the emphasis on alluvial soils, much of the steeper land in Fiji is cropped less frequently than hitherto. This reappraisal of land quality, together with the increased demands per household, may bring increased population pressure without any change in population numbers. These tendencies are common to many islands, large and small, but the consequences are felt much more quickly on the latter.

The desire to specialize in export crop production brings other difficulties to the smallest islands. Specialization in growing a commercial crop can only be realized if others specialize in food crop production and an exchange economy develops within the island. But on the very small islands though a man can specialize in copra production (for which there is an export market) no individual can specialize in taro (or other food crop) production because the local market remains too small. In effect everyone must remain a non-specialist or become a migrant. The problem of the small size of the local market also hampers the provision of many specialist services (such as medical or advanced educational facilities) on the small islands. Migration tends to result from knowledge that opportunities have increased, or are better, elsewhere rather than from declining real living standards on the home island. Felt wants rather than outright necessity stimulate migration and, as education and communications improve on the larger islands, and commercial attitudes grow stronger, the contrast in opportunities between small and large islands becomes more obvious and the incentive to migrate increases. In general, it may be that the smallest islands will cease to be viable economic units as commercial forms of economic organization increase in importance. In the case of Tokelaus, the whole population may migrate to New Zealand in the next few years.

Although the larger islands share some of the problems which threaten the economic (and demographic) stability of the small islands, their difficulties are different in kind as well as in degree. Some islands have a reserve of unoccupied land (though institutional difficulties may inhibit its use) and most are large enough to allow an internal exchange economy to flourish. Nevertheless the increases in work force which are projected (Table II) indicate that there must be considerable economic growth if present standards of living are to be maintained or improved. And the limited size of the internal markets of most of these territories limits the avenues for development. Expansion and diversification of agriculture is difficult or almost impossible for those territories which consist mainly of groups of small limestone islands or of steep, broken peaks (e.g. Tonga, Tokelaus, Niue, French Polynesia, the Northern Cooks, and the outer islands of Fiji). The others will be hard put to find additional crops which will pay. In Fiji, for example, the range of export crops has shrunk over the years. Distance from markets, world over-production, lack of interest, institutional problems, lack of capital, and numerous other economic and social difficulties have been the stumbling blocks. It would appear that an increasing proportion of the work force in all territories will have to find employment in non-agricultural occupations and at present the opportunities are limited. Undoubtedly employment in service occupations will rise with greater commercial and administrative activity, but for stability, such an increase requires parallel development in the primary and secondary sectors.

Present industrial development in Polynesia is restricted. The processing of agricultural produce for export includes sugar and copra milling in Fiji, cocoa fermenting and drying in Western Samoa, and fruit canning in Rarotonga but, with a few exceptions, most other industrial enterprises are concerned only with local markets. Most territories have timber mills, bakeries, soft drink plants, furniture manufacturers, tailors, and boat builders but apart from such ubiquitous industries (whose scope for expansion is limited) additional industries are usually based on special conditions which can scarcely be reproduced elsewhere. Only Fiji appears to have a large enough internal market to support such industries as a cement plant, brewery, cigarette and match factories, biscuit and milk-processing factories, and facilities for the repair of ships. Undoubtedly there is room for further import substitution in Fiji and also for the export of manufactured goods to other Polynesian groups. Cigarettes, beer, biscuits, and sterilized milk are already exported in small quantities. Apart from Fiji, none of the groups are large enough to support forest industries which can hope to serve more than the local market, and even this may not be fully supplied.

The prospects for territories other than Fiji developing export industries are limited. The tuna-canning plant in American Samoa (with fishing done by Japanese contractors) is dependent upon free access of its produce into the United States, an advantage which no other territory will be able to share. Nevertheless fish freezing and canning plants to serve other Pacific-margin markets might prove feasible and one such plant has recently begun operations in Fiji. The clothing factory in Rarotonga depends largely upon its low wage rates and free entry to the New Zealand market. Nearly one-eighth of Rarotonga's population depends on the factory (*Pacific Islands Monthly*, October 1962, p. 40) but significant expansion of production would meet opposition from New Zealand unions and management if any undercutting of New Zealand manufacturing costs began to threaten employment. Similarly, New Zealand citrus producers have expressed concern at the possible volume of citrus imports from the Cooks. Production of handicrafts, which provide income for the smallest territories, could be increased but not to such an extent as would restore the balance of trade. As Belshaw has said, 'by and large, to suppose that industrialization will provide a way out, following the pattern of developed economies, is a pipe dream' (1960, p. 135).

One expanding industry is tourism. It is now the third source of overseas exchange in Fiji, where the number of visitors in 1963 showed an increase of 32·8 per cent over the previous year (*News from Fiji*, 29.1.64). In French Polynesia the industry is close to outstripping the territory's declining agriculture in exchange earnings. In 1957 Tahiti had 700 visitors while in 1963, 14,155 tourists passed through the international airport (*Pacific Islands Monthly*, July 1964, p. 53). Undoubtedly other territories could do more to encourage tourism though some, such as Western Samoa, Tonga, and the Cook Islands, have had serious doubts about the effects of such development on their way of life. Until overseas capital is actively sought, as happened in Tahiti and Fiji, development is likely to be slow. Even when actively promoted the tourist industry of Polynesia will remain small compared with that of larger countries situated nearer the main sources of tourists. And like all other economic activities in Polynesia, it is an industry which is vulnerable to outside events, is liable to exhibit instability, and is likely to favour the larger rather than the smaller islands and territories.

POLITICAL CONSEQUENCES

The consequences of small size on the present political state and likely course of development in the Polynesian territories arise mainly from questions of economic viability and the provision of skilled manpower. The latter includes not only the problem of providing trained people but that of keeping them in the territory. Although small size does appear to make political advancement to full independence difficult in many respects, it may well have some advantages. For example the creation of a sense of national identity may be easier than in larger and more diverse communities. At present the political status and degree of independence enjoyed by the Polynesian territories exhibits great variety. Fiji, the largest territory, remains a colony, while Western Samoa has recently gained full independence and Tonga is a self-governing state under the protection of the United Kingdom. Even the Cook Islands are more advanced politically than Fiji. It would be unwise, therefore, to claim that size in itself will be more than one among many factors which will influence future political development. Nevertheless it is probable that some of the territories, as at present constituted, will prove too small to carry out the full range of duties and activities normally performed by fully independent states.

In recent decades many of the benefits of more developed economies, such as medical services and educational opportunities, have been introduced into Polynesia by the administering powers. The low death rates and consequent population explosions are indicative of this. Such advantages have come to be highly desired by the islanders but in the context of demographic and economic vulnerability described above, the provision of such services is likely to place heavy strains on any independent administration. Hitherto subsidies from the administering powers have helped maintain services and finance development projects. In the financial year 1963-4 the Cook Islands administration received subsidies from New Zealand totalling £774,500. This sum accounted for 52 per cent of total public expenditure and more than covered the combined expenditure on education, health, and public works (N.Z., 1964, p. 25). Although economic development is proceeding it is difficult to believe (when the total value of exports in 1963 amounted to only £834,777) that local revenue will be forthcoming to replace subsidies of this order. Cook Islanders have virtually free entry to New Zealand and the loss of subsidies and consequent fall in level of services would almost certainly stimulate further emigration. Whether a higher degree of independence than the full internal self-government (and control of spending of subsidies) to be obtained in 1965, will ever be achieved may depend on whether emigration to New Zealand continues to solve the problems of population increase and on whether financial independence can be reached. The small size of the islands, their wide dispersal, and paucity of resources make the latter unlikely and the present association with New Zealand will probably continue. American Samoa, Niue, and the Tokelaus are all in a similar position and it appears that the most likely form of political solution for these territories of under 20,000 people will be some association with the United States or New Zealand respectively. It is reasonable to assert that small size (in terms of resources and economic potential) does preclude the attainment of full independence in these territories.

The larger territories all have better prospects of becoming economically and politically viable. The Tongan budget is balanced from revenue, there is no public debt, and the equivalent of nearly two years' expenditure is invested in Commonwealth (mainly Australian) securities. Provided Tonga continues to enjoy the protection of the United Kingdom, is not required to increase expenditure on items such as defence, can maintain the financial benefits of multiple-office holding under her present form of government, and is successful in continuing her orthodox and unorthodox methods of expanding her overseas earnings,[1] there is little reason to believe that her present independence cannot be maintained. Even so, Tonga does rely on the United Kingdom's assistance in certain overseas transactions and for the provision of some skilled services. Western Samoa, larger and potentially more productive, is more recently independent but has chosen to employ New Zealand as her agent in many matters of foreign affairs. This may provide a model for the other relatively large territories of Fiji and French Polynesia. Spokesmen in the former have expressed a desire for some form of association with the United Kingdom similar to that enjoyed by the Isle of Man, but whether this is feasible between such widely separated areas is questionable.

All Polynesian territories are facing or are likely to face problems of providing a sufficiently large and skilled civil service to carry the administration of independent government. This is partially an educational problem but it is increased by the particularistic nature of many of the island societies and by the small field from which recruits may be drawn. The separation of various branches of government, often

[1] These include the minting of gold coinage and the issue of circular stamps printed on laminated gold foil to commemorate the coins. The latter earned the country revenue 'of the order of approximately £T120,000'. Government of Tonga, 1964; *Report of the Premier for the year 1963*. Nuku'alofa. In 1966 it was announced that Tonga would seek an overseas loan.

thought desirable, may well result in a disproportionate number being employed in administration in very small territories, yet in these same territories there may be insufficient work in one field to provide full employment for skilled personnel. In local administration the fragmentation of the Polynesian territories increases the difficulties. A man on one island often cannot serve the needs of another island.

Multiple office holding is one solution to the problem and is exemplified by the Tongan administration. The former Prime Minister (and then heir apparent) H.R.H. Prince Tupouto'a Tungi (now King Taufa'ahau) was the minister or ministerial head of the equivalent of at least six departments and the chairman of the produce boards controlling the marketing of export crops. The financial advantages of such a system are considerable and full use is made of trained personnel. But there are obvious dangers, for example if the holder of such a range of offices were less able. Western Samoa, with a more elaborate form of government than that of Tonga, has had difficulty providing the necessary civil servants but, following a crash training programme and attempts to provide 'a more economical and compact administrative machine . . . without loss of efficiency' (*Pacific Islands Monthly*, October 1962, p. 146), prospects now appear better.

Once men are trained for advanced posts, particularly in technical fields, the smaller territories often find difficulty in retaining them. Training must frequently be obtained outside Polynesia and acquaintance with the higher wage rates and wider employment opportunities in, say, New Zealand or the United States, reduces the attraction of returning to the home territory where outlets for skill and ability are limited. Migration is a selective process and in the Cook Islands for example, a disproportionate number of emigrants come from the better educated section of the community.

The larger Polynesian territories, and particularly Fiji, are less affected by this problem of loss of skill. The range of experience and opportunities offered within the colony are greater while emigration is less easily accomplished. Fiji residents do not enjoy easy access to any near-by country. Fiji's problems in progressing towards greater independence are likely to arise not from the size of the territory or availability of personnel but from the multi-racial society and the divergent attitudes of the several communities. It may prove difficult to forge a sense of national awareness in these circumstances. In this case the smaller territories are more fortunate. Although the present political boundaries are largely the result of actions of colonial powers rather than of internal developments, there is a high degree of cultural and linguistic unity in all territories. In recent decades inter-island movements and common administration have increased the community of interest within each territory and, in fostering this, it should be possible to turn small size to advantage.

The question remains whether or not the broad cultural unity of Polynesia might not become a basis for federation and provide a means of overcoming many of the difficulties arising from smallness. At present this seems unlikely. Some form of association between the two Samoas, separated for only sixty-five years, would outwardly appear promising. There are no language difficulties, most people of one territory have relatives living in the other, the main islands are close together and there are frequent air and sea links. But divergent economic ties (Table III), the advantages of the American link for the eastern territory, traditional rank differences between chiefs (and the probability that the Eastern Samoan chiefs would lose status) all militate against such a union. Elsewhere very great distances between islands, lack of economic interaction, and divergent ties with other states all hinder political federation. There are however some opportunities for closer economic co-operation between those territories which do lie close together. One example of this is the construction of a coconut processing plant in American Samoa to be supplied largely from Tonga but which will enjoy free access to the United States market for its produce. How far such developments can be extended depends primarily on the administering powers and as yet there is little evidence on which to base predictions of their likely attitudes.

CONCLUSION

As a result of cultural contact and economic change the importance of smallness has increased throughout Polynesia. The very small and more isolated islands have suffered most. Under a subsistence economy their smallness resulted in a more precarious existence for their inhabitants than was normal on the larger islands with a wider resource base. Overpopulation seems to have been a real and recurrent danger. Otherwise, smallness in itself did not place these islands at too great a disadvantage vis-à-vis the larger islands. But with the change to a commercial economy, population pressure has often been increased while changes in agriculture have increased vulnerability to outside forces. Desires for more individualistic forms of socio-economic organization have been introduced and the demands for more material goods and services have increased. The very small islands cannot fulfil all these new requirements. The general consequence of these changes is an increase in emigration from the smaller islands, whose ultimate role may be as sites for coconut plantations visited only occasionally from the larger islands. Such a development would take place gradually and in effect would mean the end of many small communities as separate entities.

Some islands may become sites for tourist marinas and luxury resorts[1] with their only indigenous peoples being found in 'true to life' villages maintained for the benefit of tourists dwelling in air-conditioned comfort. Such a prospect is sad, but it certainly appears that many of the smaller islands will cease to be viable socio-economic units as present trends in cultural change continue.

The larger islands have more encouraging prospects though rapidly increasing populations emphasize the vulnerability arising from limited land areas. For these islands and for the territories as units it is fragmentation, the consequent internal transport problems, and distance from world markets which make the small territories of Polynesia distinctive. Otherwise, the problems of providing skilled manpower, of encouraging economic development and diversity, and of achieving political (and economic) independence are consequences of smallness common to minor territories the world over.

[1] As Polynesian Paradise Inc. of Los Angeles hope to develop Palmyra atoll. See *Pacific Islands Monthly*, September 1962, pp. 67–9, and November 1962, pp. 56–9.

8

THE HIGH COMMISSION TERRITORIES
WITH SPECIAL REFERENCE
TO SWAZILAND[1]

J. E. Spence

SWAZILAND is an area roughly the size of Wales and bounded on the north, west and south by South African territory. Thus, unlike Basutoland, it is not entirely an island in the South African heartland and, unlike Bechuanaland, it is more compact with an area of 6,704 square miles as against the 275,000 of the former. British jurisdiction was finally confirmed in 1907 when the Territory fell under the direct control of the High Commissioner for South Africa after nearly twenty years as a pawn in the complex struggle between Boer and Britain for hegemony in Southern Africa. This conflict was to leave its mark on the territory as subsequent analysis will demonstrate.

THE DEMOGRAPHIC ASPECT

Swaziland falls into category C (thinly populated—less than 50 persons per square mile) of Mr Smith's analysis (*supra*, p. 11). The following table gives an indication of population growth over the last fifty years:

Selected census year

Group	1904	1921	1946	1956	Estimate 1961
African	84,529	110,295	181,269	233,214	260,000
European	890	2,205	3,201	5,919	9,400
Eurafrican	72	451	745	1,378	2,000
Total	85,481	112,951	185,215	240,511	271,400

Source: *Swaziland Government Report*, 1961, p. 7.

Included in the 1956 figure of 233,214 Africans were 8,048 born outside Swaziland. Although these immigrants comprised only 3·4 per cent of the 1956 total (181,269), their numbers increased by 152 per cent over the next ten years. The increase of 51,945 between 1946 and

[1] This paper was written before Basutoland and Bechuanaland became independent but some amendments have been made to take account of this.

1956 is divided between 4,854 by immigration and 47,091 by natural increase. This rise in immigration is probably explained by the widening range of employment as the economy expanded. Between 1936 and 1946 the African population increased by 18·3 per cent and by 28·6 per cent in the following decade.[1] The birth rate dropped from 53 per thousand in 1946 to 47 per thousand in 1956, while the death rate for the latter year was estimated at 26 per thousand.[2] Thus in terms of Mr Smith's analysis, Swaziland is unusual in that its annual rate of natural increase (2·8 per cent) is higher than that of most territories in List C of his paper. Nor has immigration been the main source of population growth as in some of the other small territories.

Immigration has, however, been an important factor in the rapid increase of the size of the white population of Swaziland. Between 1946 and 1956 the white population rose by 85 per cent as compared with 16·9 per cent in the previous decade, while the five-year period 1956–61 shows another sharp increase of well over 50 per cent. The bulk of this post-war rise is due to immigration, much of it from South Africa, attracted by the exploitation of Swaziland's mineral and agricultural resources and their presence in the Territory fits in with Benedict's analysis of the role of 'outsiders' in small-scale societies (*supra*, pp. 49–50). Indeed, 60 per cent of the whites of the Territory are South African born. Nevertheless it is clear that the rise in white numbers has done little to offset the Swazi majority which still outnumbers the former by 27 to 1.

The African inhabitants are essentially agriculturalists, and the land available for exclusive Swazi occupation is 3,451 square miles, carrying in 1961 a population of 228,000. As Monica Cole has pointed out in her discussion of population distribution in Southern Africa as a whole (1961, p. 660), there are no African towns or cities as such: Mbabane and Bremersdorp, the two largest urban centres, owe their existence to white economic penetration. As two authorities on the subject have pointed out (Green and Fair, 1960, p. 200), economic development has taken place in a patchwork of zones in each of which can be found a 'varying combination of mining, forestry, agriculture and irrigation, and industry, commerce and towns'.[3] This pattern was partly set by the historical division of the territory into patches of African and white

[1] The corresponding percentage increases for South Africa in the same period were 18·9 and 19·2 respectively.

[2] Registration of births and deaths is not compulsory, nor do the birth-rate figures take infant mortality into account; thus these estimates are only approximate.

[3] This confirms Mr Smith's assertion (*supra*, p. 17) that development in List C territories has been restricted largely to areas contiguous to the main town or owns.

owned land. The former is reserved exclusively for the Swazi people with the result that the bulk of economic and urban development has taken place in the white enclaves. The four main zones of development are: (a) Mbabane—Bremersdorp; (b) Piggs Peak–Lomati Valley; (c) Eranchi–Hlume; (d) Ubombo–Big Bend. More than half the white population is to be found in zones (a) and (b) while 30 per cent of the African population live in zone (a) making it the most densely populated of the four.

There is a marked contrast between development in each of these zones and that which obtains in the African areas. On the other hand, there is evidence suggesting that the inhabitants are gradually moving from a subsistence to a money economy. The Swazi, for example, now produce 18 per cent of the Territory's cotton and 40 per cent of its tobacco. In addition the 4,000 Africans who belong to farmers' associations are responsible for most of the £160,000 worth of cotton, tobacco, maize, kaffir corn, and vegetables sold in the white areas. But this contribution should be not be exaggerated; white farmers were credited in 1959 with a cash crop production worth £730,000, while only 1,000 of the 27,000 acres under irrigation are in the African areas.

Like Basutoland and Bechuanaland and other List C territories, Swaziland exports labour—in this case, to the mines, farms, and industries of the neighbouring Republic of South Africa. The average number employed in South Africa in 1961 was 10,800 (that is, 15 per cent of the adult male population), a figure which contrasts favourably with the 20 per cent and 43 per cent for Bechuanaland and Basutoland respectively. These workers made a contribution of approximately £200,000 to the Swazi economy, measured in terms of deferred pay, family remittances, and the like. The contrast with Basutoland is striking: soil erosion, primitive methods of subsistence agriculture, and a shortage of land all help explain the high proportion of Basuto males who seek work in South Africa, and the same is true to a lesser extent of Bechuanaland.

ECONOMIC ASPECTS

Discussing the future of the Territories, the 1960 Economic Survey Mission maintained that 'each Territory is in the situation of a patient confronted with a choice between having an expensive operation, which would entail a long period of recuperation but offer a high chance of full recovery, and the alternative of lapsing into a state of chronic illness' (1960, p. 14).

This diagnosis has added point when one considers Swaziland's economic potentiality and the delay in developing its resources in the ten years after 1945. In this period it received £1,100,377 from funds allocated under the Colonial Development and Welfare Act of 1945.[1] In 1955 however, the situation improved with a further CDWF grant of £1,010,239 while in the same year the Territory's first general loan was floated, amounting to £1,667,000. Four years later a further grant of £1¾ million was made available, again under the auspices of the Colonial Development Corporation. In the same period, as Green and Fair point out (1962, p. 164), a significant change in the pattern of revenue receipts occurred. By 1956 the contribution of African tax receipts to total revenue had dropped to 5 per cent;[2] by contrast receipts from Income Tax and Base Metal Royalties (chiefly from asbestos) had increased sharply. In 1958–9, for example, the former yielded £664,000, that is, 50 per cent of total revenue, and it is significant that both increases coincided with the influx of whites mentioned earlier in this paper.[3] Thus by 1960, to quote Green and Fair, 'the Colonial Development Corporation, and powerful private and public interests in the United Kingdom and the Union of South Africa had begun to participate directly in the Territory's economic affairs.' (Green and Fair, 1960, p. 195). The 1960 Mission suggested a further public investment of £2,667,260 which it argued would supply the necessary impetus for the achievement of economic viability.

No doubt it would be a mistake to regard Swaziland as an exception to Mr Knox's view that small countries tend to lack diverse resources, but what is particularly striking about the Territory is the relative wealth of its natural resources compared with those of Basutoland, Bechuanaland, and many of the territories examined by other contributors to this volume. Havelock, for example, has the world's largest asbestos mine and there appear to be significant deposits of coal and gold. In addition, iron ore mining was stimulated by the decision to build the long-awaited railway spanning the Territory from east to west. Courtaulds, assisted by the Colonial Development Corporation, have established a £10 million wood-pulp project to exploit the abundant timber resources for export to Britain and European markets.[4] Swaziland is also particularly rich in water resources and cash crops such as tobacco, citrus, and cotton are being extensively developed. Efforts have been made to persuade the Swazi, traditionally a pastoralist, to change to

[1] This, of course, represents a considerable increase as compared with expenditure in the years before 1939.

[2] In 1937 the contribution was 41 per cent and in 1946 12 per cent.

[3] One other major source of revenue remains to be mentioned, namely the £240,000 (1960 figure) derived from the customs agreement with South Africa. This is the second largest source of revenue and underlines what will be said presently about Swaziland's dependence on South Africa.

[4] The Colonial Development Corporation planted 100,000 acres of pine wood between 1948 and 1958.

arable production, although the 1960 Commission sounded a warning about the dangers of soil erosion, for decades a major problem in all three Territories.

Swaziland's pattern of international trade illustrates Mr Knox's remarks about the economic implications of smallness. The smallness of the Swazi home market and the proximity of a large rich country in South Africa makes the latter, therefore, the chief outlet for Swazi exports, including asbestos (for re-export), by far the major component of the total export figure of nearly £4 million (1958 figures), and amounting to 48 per cent of this total.[1] The fact that imports in 1958 totalled £3,161,990, revealing a marked dependence on South Africa particularly in regard to foodstuffs, raw materials, and manufactured goods of all kinds, indicates the high degree to which Swaziland depends on foreign trade with a limited range of partners to meet its requirements.

The 1960 Commission made a rough estimate of the potential increase in annual gross value of output on the following basis:

Potential increase (millions)	
Irrigation farming	£3·5 to 7·5
Forest plantations	1·0 to 1·3
Minerals (iron ore, coal)	1·5 to 2·1
Total	6·0 to 10·9

The Commission emphasized, however, that these increases would depend, inter alia, on improved communications, particularly the provision of a railway service, considerable investment in irrigation farming and forest plantations, and the capacity of existing markets to absorb increased output.

Indeed it is clear that better communications are a crucial factor in consolidating and extending such development as has taken place. The Commission, in recommending that over £2 million be spent on the necessary 'expensive operation' allocated just over half this sum to road construction and it is not difficult to see why. Green and Fair in their analysis argue that Swaziland's economic difficulties stem from its 'remoteness from the major arteries of trade, and its inaccessibility relative to those parts of the eastern watershed region which are traversed by the roads and railways serving the hubs of population and economic activity' (1960, p. 197). This situation is in stark contrast to

[1] This preponderance of asbestos supports Mr Knox's contention (supra, p. 36) that small countries tend to be more specialized than larger ones in their export trade.

that prevailing in the neighbouring Republic, where economic development has focused on 'the major ports, the major interior centres of production and the lines of communication between them' (Green and Fair, 1960, p. 195). The huge mining and industrial complex of the Witwatersrand is linked by road and rail to the ports of Lourenço Marques, Durban, East London, and Port Elizabeth. These have in turn become major industrial centres and, part cause and part effect, Africans in increasing numbers have been attracted to them to become a settled urban proletariat. Nor have inland centres failed to benefit from this network of communication; indeed most areas with natural resources have easy access to it.

Swaziland has hitherto not participated in this rapid process of industrialization, despite the fact that it lies no further than 200 miles from Johannesburg. Nor has the South African government ever been very enthusiastic about improving rail and road communications in the Territory. Its existing rail links with Lourenço Marques are satisfactory enough not to require an additional line connecting, for example, Lothair and Goba. The importance of efficient communications for Swaziland is clearly demonstrated in the Mbabane/Bremersdorp zone through which the main Territory road between the Transvaal and Mozambique passes, and which has helped the development and marketing of that area's resources. By contrast the Piggs Peak/Lomati Valley area is less fortunate. In the absence of good communications across the mountains, asbestos from the Havelock mine has to be carried by aerial ropeway to the railhead at Barbeton in the Transvaal. The extensive timber industry in this area faces a similar problem: its products are transported along a difficult road to Hectorspruit, sixty miles from Piggs Peak.

However, in 1961 a decision was taken to build a railway linking the iron ore deposits at Bomou Ridge with Goba in Mozambique. Finance for its construction was being provided by the Colonial Development Corporation and the Anglo-American Corporation in South Africa. It is significant that the crucial factor affecting the decision was the agreement signed by the Swaziland Iron Ore Development Company (an Anglo-American subsidiary) with a number of Japanese companies to supply 12 million tons of iron ore over a ten-year period beginning in 1964. It demonstrates the cardinal importance of improved communications if markets for Swaziland's products are to be found

In its report, the Survey Mission insisted that a single integrated plan be devised to cope with Swaziland's growing pains. The chief difficulty, however, is the fact that the European areas are the key growth points for the entire Territory, and it seems likely that unless positive steps are taken, these areas will soon outstrip the African ones. The Mission rightly pointed to the need to develop the latter as soon as possible in the direction of production for the market rather than for subsistence. This will clearly involve an agricultural revolution running parallel with industrial expansion, a goal which presents a number of problems.

The 1960 Report stressed that the expanding demand for labour, largely stimulated by postwar economic development, would probably continue, yet despite the fact that current (1959) requirements for the unskilled category were being met satisfactorily doubts were expressed whether this would continue to be the case. Lack of adequate training facilities accounted for a shortage of skilled and semi-skilled labour, a shortage which was likely to increase unless existing facilities were greatly improved. The Report put the number of male Swazis of wage-earning age (between 18 and 50 years) at 45,000 while both private and public employers calculated that their labour requirements would rise from 15,365 (in 1959) to 20,000 by 1962. Finally it emphasized the need for labour market surveys 'for the better execution of future development plans in both the public and private sectors'. Several factors, it continued, would have to be taken into account: (a) the extent to which the peasant farmer could be induced to leave the land and take up employment in the industrial areas; (b) the lower wage structure as compared with South Africa; (c) the fact that many Swazi workers, content with the short-term contracts provided by the large South African employers, might find a permanent wage-earning status irksome. To quote the Report, 'the Swazi labourer normally regards periodical visits to his farm or other domestic interests as having priority over the claims of his employers'.[1]

Green and Fair, writing in 1961, were more cautious however. They admitted the force of the Survey's findings, but added the rider that further comparable increases in these requirements were unlikely in the next decade, as planned capacities would have been reached and existing development have to be consolidated. Thus, according to their calculations, 51 per cent of the male labour force would still be involved in the private agricultural sector, and this implied, in their view, the institution of agricultural reform if development was to be uniform for the Swazi population as a whole.

Thus the necessary agricultural revolution basically depends on developing an effective system of agricultural education. This involves encouraging the Swazi farmer to adopt better techniques and thereby facilitate the switch from subsistence to production for the market. It

---

[1] *Economic Survey Mission*, p. 447. This point illustrates the relevance of Dr Benedict's statement (*supra*, p. 50) that 'large- or even medium-scale operations would seem to require functionally specific roles'.

also involves, *inter alia*, an improvement in existing market facilities, which, as has been stressed, depends on better communications. There is an evident danger in neglecting the development of the African areas; if this happens, . . . 'The four major zones of activity will tend to lengthen their present lead over the principally African areas, instead of forming the spearhead of a general advance and the existing sectional imbalance will grow rather than diminish' (Green and Fair, 1960, p. 204).

In conclusion, the Mission's view that economic relations between all three Territories and South Africa 'must become more numerous and complex' if their recommendations were carried out, deserves quotation. This point, the Mission argued, was particularly relevant in the context of Swaziland's water and electric power development (here South Africa is the obvious customer) and crucial in any attempt to solve the Territory's marketing difficulties. The Mission stressed the need for closer consultation with the various South African agricultural boards particularly with respect to the problem of quotas.[1] This point has obvious importance in view of the Territory's dependence on South Africa as a market for the export of crops like tobacco and sugar. Green and Fair, however, go much further and argue that Swaziland's development 'may depend very much on the degree to which its communication system and economy can be integrated into those of Southern Africa as a whole' (1960, p. 205). The Territory clearly has little alternative to South Africa as far as the export of perishable goods is concerned, and this applies equally to asbestos, Swaziland's major export. With regard to iron ore and wood pulp, however, the government has decided that the chief markets lie overseas and the road and rail system at present under construction is designed to facilitate this development. The iron ore agreement with Japan is significant in this context, particularly in view of the fact that an alternative market, and perhaps a more profitable one, might have been available in the iron and steel industries of South Africa. To date there has been no proposal to link the Havelock mine and the new railway and so reduce the Territory's dependence on South Africa as a market for the export of asbestos.

Of the three Territories, Swaziland appears to have the most promising outlook. But like many other small countries, it is heavily dependent on international trade for the satisfaction of its economic requirements, and in particular on the neighbouring Republic. Green and Fair argue that 'economic integration with South Africa need not imply a political integration which the Swazi nation opposes' (1960, p. 205).

[1] The market for sugar, for example, is limited to the quota allocated by the South African Sugar Association and the Territory's wattle production is similarly controlled.

Nevertheless while an increasing degree of economic integration with a richer and larger neighbour may be a prudent course for many small states, political considerations may dictate a search for more distant and perhaps less lucrative markets. Recent developments in Swaziland exemplify this tendency for certain of its products.

SOCIOLOGICAL ASPECTS

The presence of a white minority with established rights and property has always been a complicating factor in the Territory's history. This group has considerable vested economic interests in the mineral, industrial, and agricultural wealth of the country and not surprisingly has tended to support Sobhuza II, the Paramount Chief, and the conservative Swazi National Council.[1] Altogether the Swazi own about 2·3 million acres, while whites occupy about 1·9 million acres. This division of land ownership between Swazi and white has for many decades been a potent source of Swazi resentment and has been kept alive by the fact that many of the white landowners are absentee landlords, resident in South Africa, or Afrikaner sheep farmers from the neighbouring Transvaal, using the land for winter grazing.

A second characteristic of Swazi society (and this is true of Basutoland and Bechuanaland) is the strength of the indigenous tribal institutions. These institutions were maintained virtually intact by the British authorities until administrative reforms were tardily undertaken in the 1930s. These reforms were only completed between 1944 and 1950, some considerable time after similar reforms were carried out in the other Territories.

A third factor affecting the pace of social change in all three has been the corrosive effect of labour migration upon the fabric of tribal society. In Basutoland and Bechuanaland in particular the absence of so many of the more ambitious and energetic menfolk has made successful reform of the administrative structure difficult in the past. By the same token, any attempt to improve agricultural techniques and productivity was bound to be for a long time a frustrating enterprise. Swaziland has suffered less from this disadvantage in recent years, partly because of the relatively greater range of employment opportunities within the Territory on white farms and in local industrial enterprises. Nevertheless, the fact that Swazi tribal institutions have maintained a high degree of cohesion has made the task of Swazi 'nationalists', who wish to force the pace of political and economic change, extremely difficult. The fragmentary nature of the nationalist opposition to the

[1] The Swazi National Council consists of the Liquqo, a body of hereditary chiefs and the Llibandhla, a gathering open to any adult male and meeting once a year.

dominant conservative chiefly element, allied with a majority of the white group, has inevitably complicated Swaziland's constitutional progress. Few whites can be found in the ranks of any of the nationalist parties that have emerged in recent years and indeed these appear to have made little headway in attracting a mass Swazi following. Support for their policies comes mainly from the tiny Swazi educated elite —clerks and teachers, etc. On the other hand, nationalist prospects may improve as the Territory makes economic progress and tribal inhibitions break down under the pressure of an industrial environment. All three territories suffer from a lack of adequate educational facilities and this has had obvious implications for the slow development of nationalist movements. As the Economic Survey Mission put it, 'Until recently the lack of educational opportunities and the lack of openings appear to have reinforced each other in a vicious circle of mutually adverse reaction' (1960, p. 449). The Mission estimated that just over 50 per cent of Swazi children were at school at any one time, and this figure was not substantially larger in the other Territories. Primary school enrolments numbered 28,000 in 1958 in Swaziland, with 650 in secondary schools. All three Territories had less than a hundred students at universities.

The Mission also criticized the lack of adequate technical training facilities, pointing out that many skilled and semi-skilled posts had to be filled by workers from outside the Territory. This was also true of recruits to the teaching profession, many of whom came from South Africa, a trend which again illustrates the cogency of Dr Benedict's remarks on 'outsiders' in his paper. The Mission therefore recommended the spending of £82,000 to remedy this deficiency on the grounds that 'unless the Swazi are taught how to play their part in the development of the Territory, some of the expenditure proposed in other fields may be wasted' (1960, p. 416). It further suggested that the three Territories co-operate in improving technical education and suggested that they consider specializing in various branches to avoid an unnecessary and expensive duplication.

POLITICAL ASPECTS

Of the small territories under British rule, the Protectorates are perhaps unique. Each finds itself largely surrounded (Basutoland completely so) by the territory of a much larger, highly industrialized, and powerful state. This geographical isolation is compounded by a varying degree of economic dependence on South Africa, while the *apartheid* policy constitutes an ideological factor complicating relations between the Territories and their republican neighbour. Leo Marquard has described them as South Africa's 'colonies' (1961, p. 252) and indeed that country's claim to them has been based on the assumption that they each form an integral part of South African territory which only the accidents of history and the misplaced scruples of successive British governments have denied to their rightful rulers.

Constitutional progress has not been easy for Swaziland. By 1960 Legislative Councils had been established in both Basutoland and Bechuanaland, yet Swaziland, despite a more favourable economic position, only reached this stage in May 1963, after a good deal of wrangling among the various interests represented on the 1960 Constitutional Committee established to devise an acceptable constitition. It is significant that the Swazi Progressive Party withdrew from this Committee's deliberations, the findings of which eventually proved unacceptable to the British government. What particularly irritated the Progressive leaders and, it has been claimed, the local British officials, was the provision for separate and equal representation of the two racial groups, and the fact that the twelve Swazi representatives were to be nominated by the Swazi National Council, an organization representing the Chiefs and hence more conservative views.

In May 1963 the British government devised and imposed a Constitution providing for 24 elected and 4 official members. Of the former 8 were to be Swazi, nominated by the National Council according to traditional practice; included also in this figure were 8 whites, of whom 4 were to be elected by voters on the white electoral roll and four by voters on the national roll. Finally 8 seats were to be filled by persons of any race and elected by voters on the national roll.

None of the Swazi political parties found these proposals satisfactory however. What was particularly resented was the unwillingness of the British Government to concede the principle of majority rule as a basis for constitutional discussion. Elections were held in July, 1964, resulting in an overwhelming victory for the Royalist Imbokodvo Party which captured 16 of the 24 elected seats, the remainder going to the Conservative United Swaziland Association representing white interests. It will be clear from this brief analysis that the presence of an economically powerful white minority complicates Swazi constitutional development to an extent that has not been true of the other Territories. Yet if economic viability were the sole criterion Swaziland would have been the most obvious candidate for independence.

THE EXTERNAL SITUATION

Allied to uncertainty about Swaziland's constitutional future is the difficult problem (applying to all three Territories) of Swaziland's political relations with South Africa. South African motives for incorporation need not concern us, except incidentally. It is enough to say that since 1948 successive Nationalist victories at the polls and a Statute Book bulging with discriminatory legislation have aroused concern both in the United Kingdom and in the Territories about the latter's future. These fears were further stimulated by the report of the Tomlinson Commission in 1956, which set out in great detail a blueprint for the development of the so-called Bantustans in which the policy of separate development would find its ultimate political and economic fulfilment. Nationalist supporters acclaimed this document as demonstrating once and for all their party's sincerity in trying to find a workable and honest solution for the hitherto intractable 'native problem'. However, the politically conscious among the inhabitants of the Territories no less than interested parties in Britain and elsewhere viewed with alarm the report's finding that the incorporation of the three Territories was essential if the Bantustan programme was to have a chance of lasting success.

Since 1960, however, the Territories have acquired new significance for South African policy. All three have become staging posts for political refugees escaping from the Republic and privileged sanctuaries for members of banned political organizations in South Africa. The government has reacted by enforcing strict border controls and is no doubt aware of the Territories' vulnerability to South African counter pressure should they acquire any real significance for Pan African attempts at 'liberation'. Nor is it likely that the Territories could be safeguarded against the effects of economic sanctions by the Western powers against the Republic and this makes them valuable hostages for the South African government in its efforts to stave off direct action of this kind.

It is doubtful whether the South African government seriously entertains any hope of incorporation by agreement with the United Kingdom. This was admitted by Dr Verwoerd, the late Prime Minister, in 1961, although a year later he challenged the British Government to let him explain to the inhabitants the advantages which would follow from their administration as an integral part of the Bantustan scheme. More recently, in 1964, he has referred to the advantages the Territories might receive from a 'Common Market' embracing Southern Africa as a whole 'in which none of the member nations would have political control of any of the others but in which all would co-operate to their mutual benefit' (*Johannesburg Star*, 29.8.64). These proposals are not without appeal to the white minority in Swaziland and Mr C. F. Todd, then Chairman of the European Advisory Council, supported Dr Verwoerd's 1961 suggestion while the *Johannesburg Star* claimed that certain chiefs and traditionalists might welcome the South African plan if only because they fear the local radical movements with their emphasis on the one man, one vote principle.[1]

It seems unlikely, however, that any of these proposals will have much effect on the political leadership in the Territories and this applies no less to the conservative Swazi hierarchy. At present the Swazi appear to be intent on advancing to independent status before committing themselves to any discussion of a closer relationship with the Republic. Nor should it be taken for granted that the Swazi leaders will take kindly to further economic integration of the kind suggested by Green and Fair in their analysis. They may have to accept the existing pattern of integration and even this assumes the triumph of economic realities over deeply felt nationalist aspirations. They probably will accept the necessity of co-existence with South Africa in the post-independence period, but they are bound to be cautious about any proposal that gives the South African government a greater influence on their affairs than it at present possesses and this would be the inevitable result of an increased degree of economic integration.

Nor can the influence of Pan-African ideology be left out of account. Its role in Swaziland seems marginal at present, particularly in view of the apparent weakness of the divided Swazi nationalist movement. It would, however, be foolish to assume that this will always be the case particularly if the Territory develops economically and traditional bonds begin to weaken. It is perhaps significant that the National Liberatory Congress, a breakaway party from the SPP, is, together with parties from Lesotho and Botswana, a member of PAFMESCA (the Pan-African Freedom Movement for East, South and Central Africa) and its subsidiary PASCO (Pan-African Solidarity Conference for Basutoland, Bechuanaland and Swaziland).

A federation of the three has never been seriously considered. This is hardly surprising given the physical difficulties of communications and the fact that each is inhabited by a people with a distinct social tradition and historical experience. Even if a Federal solution were possible, the problem of South African relations would still remain, possibly in an intensified form. By the same token, a 'special relationship' with South Africa of the kind described by Dr Wood in his discussion of Western Samoa and New Zealand is unthinkable in present circumstances. Thus three of the possible solutions put forward by Dr Wood in his paper—integration, either political or economic, federalism, and a 'special relationship'—seem to be ruled out.

These difficulties have placed the British government in an acute

[1] Editorial in *Johannesburg Star* 7.9.63. N.B. The Transkei Bantustan constitution entrenches the chiefly element by giving it a majority over the elected representation.

dilemma. Over the past few years the Territory has been making progress however uneven towards full responsibility for its internal affairs, and the scale of financial aid for economic development has been increased to the tune of £1,800,000 per annum for each. Swaziland has, at this stage, some prospect of becoming self-supporting, although even its long-awaited new railway line to Lourenço Marques depends in the last analysis on Portuguese co-operation in Mozambique. Clearly, however, the demand for full independence is bound to grow and under these circumstances British withdrawal might involve awkward consequences for all the parties concerned. Left to themselves with the shell of political independence empty of the substance of economic viability, South African pressures *might* increase against all three. A cut-off in South Africa's labour demand or a refusal to buy their exports, in the event of hostile activity directed against the Republic by irredentist groups, would have obviously severe implications for their economic well-being. This assumes that South Africa has alternative sources for meeting her labour requirements, but it is difficult to give a precise answer in this context. Nevertheless, the threat of economic strangulation cannot be lightly dismissed, and no doubt Mr Vorster is aware of his legal rights to restrict the flow of foreign labour into South Africa.

One possible solution to the problem that has been suggested assumes the granting of full independence and the establishment of close military and economic ties between Britain and her erstwhile wards. This, it is argued, would deter an expansionist policy on the part of the South African government, but on the other hand it would still leave Britain facing the risk of a headlong military clash with the Republic should extreme elements within the Territories provoke the Republic into retaliation. No doubt there are some, with strong Pan-African sympathies, who might welcome the possibility of such a clash if only because it might open the door to effective United Nations interference and the ultimate downfall of the present South African government. Whether the short-term interests of the Territories would be served, however, is decidedly open to question. In any case the scheme begs a number of vital questions: (a) the logistic and strategic problems involved both for Britain and the UN in intervention of this kind and (b) the effects on white South African opinion, which for years has been indoctrinated with an ideology which equates a last ditch stand with the survival of Western civilization in Africa.

A variation on this solution would involve giving Swaziland full powers of internal government, reserving defence and foreign policy to the British government (Wood, *supra*, pp. 26–27). This is an attractive possibility if only because it might relieve Britain of some of the dangers inherent in the arrangement described in the previous paragraph. But again, this scheme assumes that nationalist leaders would be prepared to settle for substantially less than their counterparts elsewhere in Africa, and in particular membership of the United Nations. As far as Swaziland is concerned this solution appears to be ruled out for its leaders have made no secret of their desire for independence and it would be difficult for the United Kingdom to refuse their demands having created a precedent with the other two.

One other possibility remains—the establishment in the Territories of a UN 'presence' as a tangible reminder to the Republican authorities that the integrity of the Territories is guaranteed by the Charter against external interference. How useful this would be is open to question: the South African government is unlikely physically to attack them except in the direst emergency such as civil war in South Africa brought on by United Nations sanctions or guerrilla fighting in the Republic aided and abetted by elements in the Territories. In these circumstances the token UN force would be unlikely to deter the South African government. In any case, there is a range of responses short of open hostilities available to the South African government—a cut-off in labour supply, for example—which a United Nations 'presence' could do nothing to prevent.

It is clear from this analysis that the development of the Territories has been affected by their smallness, particularly in an economic context. Indeed, their dependence on South Africa is in each case a function of their relative lack of resources and their inability to diversify their economies and trading outlets. Political factors have, however, made impossible their development as an integral part of a wider South African economic framework which in an ideal world might be the most satisfactory solution. Fear of South African influence and hostility to its racial policies has compounded with nationalist feeling to produce a situation in which political aspirations are sharply at odds with economic realities and there are at present no indications that this contradiction will easily resolve itself. And in some fields, as this paper has tried to demonstrate, economic development may well make the Territories even more dependent on South Africa than has hitherto been the case. Finally, even if we assume the collapse of white rule in the Republic and the establishment of an African government, we cannot be sure that the Territories will opt for incorporation with their larger neighbour. Independence once gained is not lightly cast aside as events elsewhere on the continent amply demonstrate.

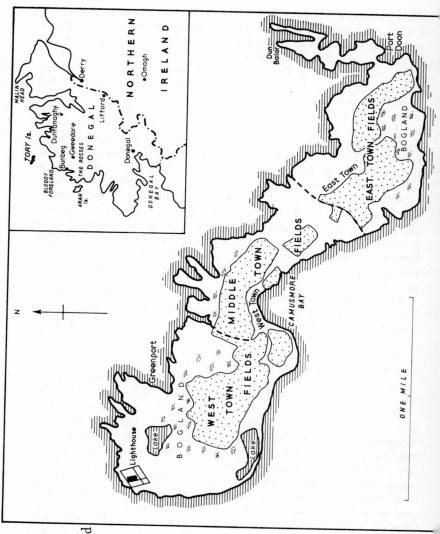

Tory Island

ONE MILE

9

TORY ISLAND¹

J. R. Fox

INTRODUCTION

Tory Island² is not a 'territory' in the sense in which the word is generally used (in fact it is technically a subdivision of a parish), but many of its problems are strikingly like those of a small territory, especially one that depends largely on migrant labour for its income, is a one-crop economy, and is heavily subsidized by a parent power. So special are the island's problems compared with those of a mainland parish that it is possible to treat it as a separate entity for analytical purposes. In political terms, however, it does not have quite the same problems as territories proper—it is simply part of the Republic of Ireland (Eire). I have not therefore dealt with political problems here.

What may come out of a comparison of Tory with other small territories is, I hope, a wider understanding of the problems of such small and vulnerable entities when they become involved in the affairs and economies of the wider world, and when they try to push up their standards of living to match those of more prosperous areas. As far as the Irish government is concerned it would be advantageous for the island to be self-supporting. At the moment it is heavily subsidized. In this respect alone it bears a resemblance to some small territories.

¹ The research on which this paper is based (and which is still intermittently in progress) has been supported by the University of Exeter, and the Anthropological and Geographical Research division of the London School of Economics. So many individuals have helped in various ways that it would be impossible to list them all. May I therefore thank collectively all those concerned from Tory itself and from the following institutions and departments: Folklore Commission; Ministry of the Gaeltacht; Land Commission, Valuation Office, Central Statistics Office, Ordnance Survey, and National Library—Dublin; Land Registry and County Library—Donegal; Trinity College, Dublin, and University College Dublin. I must single out for special thanks Séamus Ó Raghallaigh (Dunfanaghy), Ed. R. O'Connor (U.S. Embassy, Dublin), and Wynn Lewis (London School of Economics).

² Pronounced 'Torry' and so written on some older maps [from the Gaelic TORACH or TORAIGH]. It is thought that tóraidhe—'robber'—is the most likely source of the name, as the island was traditionally the home of giants who raided the mainland. The epithet 'tory' in English politics is derived from this same word. In this article I have stuck to standard anglicizations to save confusion, although these often do violence to the Gaelic originals.

The historical survey that follows is somewhat impressionistic, as I have been faced with gaps in the documentation and the lapses of informant memory. Also, there are probably large numbers of documents which I have not yet examined, and a great deal of documentation (as I have learned already) is not of the kind that is most useful in reconstructing the social structure of the past.[1]

LOCATION AND SETTLEMENT

Tory is an island of Gaelic-speaking Roman Catholics, nine miles' journey by sea from the north-west coast of Donegal (Bloody Foreland) over a rough channel. (See Map.) An open motor-boat from the island is supposed to make three runs a week for mail, but the number of runs varies greatly, depending on the weather. Every fortnight, weather permitting, a boat from Bunbeg brings stores and relief for the lighthouse and will carry stores for the islanders. In anything but very calm weather, which is rare, the passage is dangerous, so the island is easily cut off.[2] Sometimes there is no contact with the mainland for six or eight weeks in the winter. In 1960 the Christmas mail arrived in February. On some occasions the Aran lifeboat has had to be called out to bring serious medical cases off the island, and on one occasion an R.A.F. helicopter was called in. Most of the boats, which the islanders usually build themselves with great skill, are motor powered, but often with converted car engines which are unreliable. Every boat still carries sail, and with a good wind the journey can be quicker by sail than by motor. Even so, the island is now infinitely more accessible than in the days of small two-man canoes and skiffs, when the isolation must have been extreme.

The island is roughly two and a half miles long and averages about a quarter of a mile wide. It slopes upwards to the north and this shelving effect is what makes it habitable. The small areas of arable land are protected from the worst ravages of the Atlantic by the cliffs which rise to nearly three hundred feet at the eastern end. These cliffs are eaten into by fjord-like inlets of spectacular beauty. Most of them are useless as harbours, and there is in fact only one good harbour on the island, in Camusmore Bay at West Town. At Port Doon and Greenport at the western and eastern ends, there are passable landing places. The arable soil is concentrated in two main areas each of which has become the focus of a settlement. The two 'towns' (bailte) are known respectively as West Town (Baile Thiar) and East Town (Baile Thoir). West Town

[1] When speaking of the present here I am referring to 1960-5.
[2] The rating valuation records have been virtually unrevised since 1917, and for year after year one finds such entries as 'unable to inspect because of bad weather'. (Records in the Valuation Office, Dublin.)

is usually also divided into West Town proper, Middle Town (*Baile Lár*)—a long-standing division—and New Town (*Baile Úr*)—a more recent 'ribbon' development along the road from west to east. On the far west there is the complex of buildings around the lighthouse, and at Dún Balór in the east, the remains of an old hill fort (Sidebotham, 1949).

The two settlements are very different. There are 42 inhabited houses in West Town and only 24 in East Town. West Town has all the amenities. Here are the Church, national school, dance hall (a one-time co-operative store), post-office, dispensary, pier and slipways, three shops, graveyard, and life-saving station. This is the metropolis. The East, in contrast, is 'rural' with no official shops or other amenities. Nevertheless its inhabitants are fiercely loyal to it and praise its healthy atmosphere, the quietness, and above all the friendliness of the place. This contrasts with the bustle and relative impersonality of the 'town'. The West Town people take the opposite view. They like the bustle and activity and regard the East as 'lonely'. Some Westerners have never been to the East and declare they would die if they had to live there. The towns are not more than half a mile apart.

POPULATION

There is some difficulty in establishing the 'real' population of Tory as it is subject to fluctuations resulting from the absence of migrant workers for long periods. There tends to be a wave of young people returning home in the summer, and another slight increase at the time of the Scottish new year celebrations—weather permitting. The official census figures for 1961 give 146 males and 118 females; a total of 264.[1] This census was taken in the autumn and so probably represents a fair average figure: it would be higher during the summer and lower in the winter.

The gradual decline of Tory population is shown in Table I. The island has declined to roughly two thirds of its 1841 population.[2] The loss of females is most spectacular, their number being practically halved. The drop of 50 males between 1861 and 1871 was probably a result of emigration, and the drop of 41 females between 1901 and 1911 may have been the result of both emigration and a measles epidemic. The total drop between 1911 and 1926 (57) is said to have been a result of panic emigration at the beginning of World War I, when it was feared that able-bodied men might be conscripted. (Some of these

[1] Figures supplied by the Central Statistics Office, Dublin Castle.
[2] This compares with the drop in population for Ireland as a whole, from 6,548,000 in 1841, to 2,818,000 in 1961; a loss of more than half.

returned later.) Since that time the population has remained fairly
steady.

TABLE I. Tory Island population
(census returns 1841–1961)

	Male	Female	Total
1841	191	208	399
1851	207	195	402
1861	201	185	386
1871	151	192	343
1881	140	192	332
1891	160	188	348
1901	149	186	335
1911	162	145	307
1926	134	116	250
1936	147	144	291
1946	141	124	265
1951	143	114	257
1956	148	125	273
1961	146	118	264

Source: Central Statistics Office, Dublin.
Note: Figures include a few non-permanent residents such as the priest and
lighthousemen.

If we compare the population pyramids for 1901 (the first available
breakdown by age and sex) and 1961, the radical change in the age–sex
structure of the island becomes graphically apparent. (See Figure.)
An increase in the number of old people is matched by a severe decline
in the number of the working population, particularly young women.
Indeed, in 1961, for the 20–24 age group there were no women. This
reflects the growing tendency of women to migrate, and sometimes to
emigrate for good, especially on marriage. Young girl migrants usually
take jobs that require them to be away for most of the year, and hence
will not figure on the census returns.

This illustrates again the difficulty of arriving at an estimate of the
'effective' population which besets anyone dealing with a migrant
labour situation. But the decline is in many senses a real one and is
reflected by the figures for marriage on and off the island. As a general
rule, those islanders who marry away from the island never return to
it as permanent residents. This is particularly true of women. Table II
shows the number of marriages of people born on the island which
were solemnized on or off the island. Glasgow, Omagh and Edinburgh
were the most popular places for marriage off the island. Nineteen of
the twenty-eight marriages were of women to non-island men. Thus

there is a progressive loss of marriageable women which set in during the war and accelerated after it.

TABLE II. Marriages of persons born
on Tory (by decades)

| | Solemnized | | Total |
	On Tory	Elsewhere	
1918–27	16	0	16
1928–37	15	1	16
1938–47	19	3	22
1948–57	14	17	31
1958–64	4	7	11
Total	68	28	96

Source: Marriage and Baptismal records, St Colmcille's Church, Tory Island.
Note: The record of marriages off the island is compiled from notes added to entries in the baptismal register. These give the date, parish, and names of the parties concerned in a marriage of a Tory parishioner which is solemnized elsewhere. There may be some omissions but the overall trend is obvious.

This decline in the relative numbers of women is made worse by a natural imbalance which occurred in the decade 1947–56. Table III shows the number of births (male and female) by decades from 1897.

FIGURE I. Population of Tory Island by age and sex

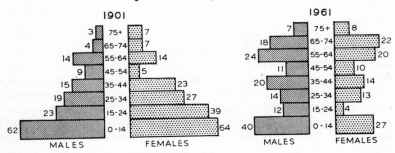

Source: Central Statistics Office, Dublin.

The ratio of males to females which had been fairly steady until 1947 suddenly swung in the male favour and produced more than two males to each female. This makes it unlikely that the men born in this period will marry on the island when they reach marriageable age. If one adds to this natural imbalance the fact that most of the marriageable girls now leave for most of the year and thus increase their chances of finding husbands off the island, then the prospects for future island marriages look bleak.

TABLE III. Tory Island births (by decades)

	Male	Female	Total	Male : Female
1897–1906	44	33	77	1 : 0·75
1907–16	18	25	43	1 : 1·3
1917–26	31	28	59	1 : 0·9
1927–36	19	25	44	1 : 1·3
1937–46	15	16	31	1 : 1·06
1947–56	32	14	46	1 : 0·4
1957–64	22	22	44	1 : 1

Source: Baptismal records, St Colmcille's Church, Tory Island.
Note: As this records only baptisms, it takes no account of infant mortality, the details of which were not available at the time of writing.

In terms of net reproduction the island more than holds its own. Between 1951 and 1961 the ratio of births to deaths was 1.6.[1] But emigration—mainly in the form of marrying away by the young women —steadily erodes the island population, and more importantly, undermines its chances of survival.

HISTORY

To understand fully the effects of migration and the growing involvement of Tory with the outside world, we have to look at its development over at least the last 150 years. Data on early Tory history is scarce. It has a great legendary past in the stories of Balór, the Fomorian giant who ruled the island and terrorized the mainland before the coming of the Gaels. He was supplanted ideologically by St Colmcille (Columba), 521–97, who is supposed to have driven off the Danes, Christianized the island, and built a monastery there. During his regime and for a time afterwards, Tory was a centre of Christian scholarship. A sense of continuity with this time is still maintained in the legend of the Duggan family—still one of the more numerous on Tory. It was a Duggan (Ó Dubhgain) who helped Colmcille to land after he had been repulsed several times. In return for this the saint granted 'the eldest Duggan' certain privileges regarding sacred relics which are maintained to this day. After this period Tory plunges again into oblivion, and the *Annals of Ulster* only give us enigmatic glances of shipwrecks and 'devastations' between A.D. 600 and 1517 (Hennessy, 1887). It reappears in 1594–1603 during the Tyrone war and the aftermath of the Armada, when it was plundered by Bingham, President of Con-

[1] Figures supplied by the Central Statistics Office.

naught (O'Donovan, 1851). (The islanders believe that many of them are descended from survivors of the Armada who were sheltered on Tory.) Again oblivion descends, until 1653, when the island is mentioned in Sir William Petty's *Civil Survey of Ireland*, as having a garrison and being under the ownership of the co-heirs of one Captain John Standford 'English Protestant: deceased'.[1] Again there is a long period of official silence until the beginning of the nineteenth century, when a lighthouse was built, and later a Lloyd's signal station.

A significant event was the purchase of the island in 1861 by a Manchester business man, Benjamin St John B. Joule.[2] The previous owner, John O. Woodhouse, Esq., must have been something of an 'improving' landlord, as the Ordnance Survey and Land Valuation Maps[3] show that between 1848 and 1858 the scattered holdings of the islanders had been consolidated into neat 'strips', something on the lines of Lord George Hill's famous reforms in Gweedore (Hill, 1868). However, Tory can never have been a very lucrative proposition as regards rents which were very difficult to collect. It is doubtful if Joule ever collected rents from the island after about 1872. In 1883 he published a remarkable pamphlet to defend himself against accusations of cruelty and indifference to his starving tenants.[4] The pamphlet consisted of reprints of letters to the press by the Rev. James J. O'Donnell, resident priest of Tory; Joule himself; and one letter ostensibly from the islanders themselves (the 'Torroneans') but probably, as Joule scornfully suggests, written by the priest. O'Donnell had appealed for funds to save the islanders from starvation, and Joule answered that this was a typical Hibernian swindle as the islanders were (a) well off from the sales of lobsters and crabs; (b) able to pay rent but had refused to do so (they were £2,000 in arrears); (c) stripping the sods from the pasture to provide fuel for illicit whiskey distilling; and (d) putting stones in kelp and selling this at inflated prices. The islanders replied that they received little

---

[1] Robert C. Simmington, ed., *The Civil Survey of Ireland*, vol. iii, Irish Manuscripts Commission, Dublin, 1931. (This followed on the 'plantation' of Ulster, 1608–20, when the Catholic Irish owners of the land were dispossessed in favour of English and Scots Protestants.)

[2] de Burgh in *The Landowners of Ireland* (1878), p. 240, lists Joule as owning 4,168 acres at an annual value of £244. Details of the purchase by Joule from Woodhouse are with the Registry of Deeds, Dublin. Joule paid £6,500 for Tory, some other islands, and a slice of the mainland.

[3] In the Valuation Office, Dublin.

[4] *Tory Island Letters*, by the Rev. James J. O'Donnell, C.C., Resident Priest of Tory, 'The Torroneans', and B. St J. B. Joule, J.P. for the County of Lancaster, etc. Rothesay, no date. The only copy I know of is in the British Library of Political and Economic Science, London School of Economics. There is no date, but it is clearly 1883, and although the publisher is not given, it would appear to be Joule, who lived in Rothesay and who added footnotes on some points.

for the crabs and lobsters. Joule's estimate had been £600 for 1882: the islanders would only admit to £35 12s per house. They maintained that they had offered a rent settlement which had been refused: they offered Joule £100 per annum instead of the £196 he was asking. They had, they said, ceased distilling illicit whiskey—a rejoinder which caused Joule much amusement. The price of kelp had dropped in their version and in 1882 they received only 18s 4d for it; Joule had estimated £700 for 1881. Clearly there are wide discrepancies here, and each side is probably exaggerating its case; but this debate—which has many interesting points that we cannot enter into here—throws a fascinating light on conditions on Tory in the latter half of the nineteenth century.

It is clear that the islanders refused to pay rates as well as rent. The 'collector of county cess' was driven off the island in 1871, and at Lifford Assizes it was decided that armed force should be used to collect the arrears (£263 15s 8d). This was more easily said than done, and it was not until 1884 (the year after the pamphlet) and probably at Joule's urgings, that the expedition was mounted. A gunboat, the *Wasp*, was dispatched from Westport, Co. Mayo, on 22 September of that year. According to Admiralty records the *Wasp* was wrecked in Tory Sound because of a 'navigational error', but the islanders maintain that they 'turned the cursing stone' on the boat. More than fifty lives were lost in this venture, and after that Joule made no further attempt to collect his rents and the county abandoned its rates. In 1903 the island was purchased by the Congested Districts Board for Ireland. Their records confirm that the islanders were 'in occupation without paying rent since about 1878'.[1] All this is important because it is a measure of the relative autonomy of the island. The islanders are proud of this autonomy and sensitive to outside interference. Their boast is that only on Tory did the potato not fail during the great famine years in Donegal (1845-9), and Tory alone did not need relief or suffer starvation. (Needless to say this was because of immunity conferred by Colmcille.) This sense of autonomy extends to dealings with the Church, and the islanders are resentful if clerical authority oversteps what they see as its legitimate limits. Even the priest should not 'go against the custom of the island'.

Since the turn of the century Tory has entered more into the mainstream of Irish life. The Congested Districts Board built houses, a pier and slipway, and made loans to develop fishing, and for a time Tory prospered (Micks, 1925). To understand this prosperity and its fluctuations we have to look at the ecology and economy of the island.

[1] Records kept by the Land Commission, Dublin.

ECOLOGY AND ECONOMY

For most of Tory's history the problem of sheer physical survival must have been uppermost. A population of over 400 crowded on to this shelf of rock, supporting itself at subsistence level from sea, shore, and farmland. The sea was limitless and there was room for all to fish, but the little two-man canoe (*curragh*) which was the standard vessel was unsuitable for deep-sea fishing and dangerous in bad weather. The cost in human life was high and the returns negligible. The fish, however, did enable the islanders to survive when many on the mainland starved. As Joule's pamphlet shows, there was some trade in lobsters and crabs which were sold to coastal steamers and taken to Liverpool. Whether this trade realized the relatively large profits—over any long period—that Joule mentions is doubtful. No large-scale fishing industry, however, could be developed on the basis of the *curragh*, and the building of larger boats required capital. A few yawls were built from imported timber at the end of the nineteenth century, but it was not until the Congested Districts Board instituted loans for fishermen that fishing really got under way. About the turn of the century large (up to 30ft) sail and oar-powered herring-fishing boats began to be built, and fishing for profit began. These boats required large crews and kept most of the able-bodied men occupied. A group of men would form a small syndicate to run a boat on a profit-sharing basis with one man as 'manager'. About eight boats were at one time in use with an average crew of nine or ten men. According to the 1901 census (see Figure I) this must have stretched the manpower resources to the full, there being certainly not more than 60–80 men and boys of working age available. Many things still made fishing difficult, not least the uncertainty of the market. Landing the fish on the mainland was always a problem, and there are many stories of wasted catches. Sometimes, in calm weather, it was necessary to row catches as far as forty miles to find a suitable market. Fresh fish were never much of a success, and it took the establishment of a curing station on the island by the Congested Districts Board to make a success of the industry. Women found employment gutting and salting herring, shops made their appearance, for a time at least Tory prospered—by Irish standards.

However, the herring were uncertain and the first World War intervened. As early as 1917 a motor-powered boat had been built on the island with capital accumulated from the fishing. After the war motor-boats became more common, and in the 1930s the Sea Fisheries Board (*Bórd Iascaigh Mhára*) provided two 'bollanders' under the management of islanders. The motors made large crews of oarsmen redundant, and drove some men to migrate. Also, after a brief season of success with 'matje' herring (a non-breeding variety that grows very fat) in the early thirties, the herring failed completely. Migrant labouring with summer fishing then became the dominant pattern of the economy.

People had always emigrated from Tory. There is not a household that does not have relatives in America, Australia, Canada, or Britain. In fact the island was something of an entrepôt in the emigration trade (Mac Gabhann, 1959, p. 86). But Tory had never been much involved in the summer migrations to Scotland and England for harvesting which characterized the rest of Donegal. However, during the first World War men took to going off for fairly long periods to gather capital for boats and equipment. They were mostly employed on public works in Scotland. Gradually truly *migrant* labouring became established. The periods abroad became shorter. At one time, men would stay away working for anything up to fifteen years—starting at 15–18— finally returning to settle down and marry at about 30. (There would have been brief excursions home for holidays during this period.) The average period of exile gradually shortened to two or three years, with brothers or cousins taking it in turn to be away. The exploitation of the lobster market altered this pattern still further, and after World War II began to dominate the economy. The lobster season is convenient in that it coincides with the summer home-coming period of the men, and is relatively short (June–September). The return is higher relative to the effort and investment than in other forms of fishing. The lobsters can be stored in floating boxes with their claws disabled to prevent fighting, and so preserved fresh for the market in a way impossible with fish. The fishing is done in two or three daily trips to lower and raise pots and does not require long journeys to sea. The motor-powered boats are efficient and require only a small crew. The fishing can be done from quite small skiffs powered by outboard motors if the weather is good.[1]

Thus it became possible for men to leave the island and work in the winter, returning home in the summer for the lobster fishing. One member of the 'crew' (usually a group of brothers or paternal cousins) remains behind to care for the boat and gear. Sometimes he is a permanent islander (if, for example, he is a shopowner), or otherwise they rotate and the 'old one'—father or grandfather of the crew—looks after the boat in the winter.

The economy of lobster fishing, while attractive, is precarious. It requires a fairly high capital investment and the risk of total loss over a

[1] It is worth noting that other forms of fishing have not completely stopped. Several non-migrant men run one quite successful herring and salmon boat. Market fluctuations and salmon gluts in recent years have however made this less successful than lobstering.

season is discouraging. A gale can take away most of the pots, lines, floats, etc. This is offset to some extent by the fact that merchants are willing to let the islanders have pots in return for a monopoly of the catch. But it holds up the fishing and can ruin a season's work. Work in Scotland in the winter is then essential in order to provide new equipment. The actual cost of petrol, oilskins, rope, etc. is often barely covered by earnings. One suspects that the attraction of lobster fishing lies not so much in its economic as its social advantages, in that the lobster/labouring complex provides a self-sustaining cycle of migration which suits the taste of the young men.

Table IV shows the involvement of households in migrant labour and fishing (and/or ferrying). As all shopkeepers have boats, the figures for boatmen include shopowners. Thus at least a third of the households have active or intermittent migrant labourers, and a third also have interests in shops and/or fishing. There is a good deal of overlap between these two groups, and between them they account for about half the households. The rest—largely consisting of older people or chronic non-migrants—live on subsidies in the form of pensions, unemployment benefits, remittances from relatives, and hidden subsidies of various kinds.

TABLE IV. Households having at least one migrant, boatman, or shopkeeper

| | Total Households | Households with: | | | |
| | | Migrants | | Boatmen shopowners | |
		Active	Intermittent	Active	Intermittent
East Town	24	5	2	6	2
West Town	42	16	3	14	4
Total	66	21	5	20	6

Source: Author's fieldnotes.
Note: 'Boatmen' is used rather than simply 'fishermen' as some men employed on boats are employed for ferrying, collecting mail, etc. The 1961 Census lists 78 adult males as 'fishermen', which works out as exactly 3 per household involved.

As well as the sea and the earnings from migrant labouring the islanders have always had their land. This has provided subsistence but little more. Perhaps at the very outside some 250 of the island's 785 acres are suitable for crops and pasture for cattle. Sheep can graze on the hillsides fairly successfully. The first Ordnance Survey map of 1835 shows that farming had been pushed to its absolute limits, field boundaries extending into what is now bog and hill-grazing land. The Tithe Aplottment Rolls of about the same period show 50 landholders with a total of about 400 acres on which tithes were levied.[1] This gives an average holding of 8 acres, but the vast majority of this was 'number two' quality land—rough grazing, commonage, bogland, etc. The amount of cultivated land and good pasture was less than this. The rating valuations of 1857 show some 60 tenants with approximately 250 acres (excluding commonage); an average of about 4 acres. The Congested Districts Board records of 1903 show 69 tenants with 233 acres (excluding commonage); an average of about 3 acres. In 1911–12 some 26 tenants registered their land, and this again shows an average holding of 3 acres. The agricultural census for 1961 however, shows that only 160 acres were in holdings and only 26 of these were under cultivation, with 34 as pasture.[2] It is difficult to calculate the exact number of holders as a number of holdings are in transition, but it is well over 70, which means that the average size of holdings has shrunk to very small proportions.

The above facts show that (a) the holdings are tiny, and (b) the area of land in use has been shrinking from a maximum use including all marginal land in 1830, to relative neglect today. In the past every scrap of usable land was of value. At one time over 200 sheep grazed on the island hills and a shepherd was jointly employed by the islanders to look after them (Swan, 1955). In 1961 there were a mere 21. There are no longer any pigs or goats. Oats, potatoes and barley are the chief crops, and very few vegetables are grown.

Until the landlord began his reforms in the 1830s and 40s, land was held on the *rundale* system (McCourt, 1955; Fox, 1966). Each town— West, Middle, and East—had a certain amount of land allotted to it, and the household heads of the town had rights to portions of the various qualities of land in the allotment. All this was under the control of the landlord or his steward, although, as we have seen, this control cannot have been very strict on Tory. In the primary valuations of land in Ireland for rating purposes (1857) we see the full effect of the reforms.[3] The land has been consolidated into strips and blocks and, although some pieces are under joint tenantship, the individual tenancy of strips is more common. With the passing of the landlords, this tenancy became virtual ownership of the strip and consequently a different pattern of land-holding predominated. The consolidated areas

[1] In the Public Records Office, The Four Courts, Dublin.
[2] Figures for 1903 from the Land Registry, Lifford. Figures for 1961 supplied by the Central Statistics Office. There is a problem in handling the acreages as the sets of units are not uniform. Sometimes land and houses are included under 'holdings', sometimes they are excluded. It might be possible by patient sifting to get more exact figures, but for present purposes the rough guide given here suffices. The overall trend is obvious enough.
[3] Maps with the Valuation Office.

became subdivided on the death of the 'owners' because of the firm
Tory belief that all children had a right to inherit. This also led to the
inevitable quarrels over the disposal of land, and a pattern of dispersed
holdings as a result of bilateral inheritance. There are several instances
of men marrying into the island because a woman had land there.

With the division of the land went the division of the peat bogs,
although these are now practically exhausted. Both the burning of kelp
and the distilling of poteen (illicit whiskey) have been blamed for this.
Kelp burning was at one time a major occupation. This type of seaweed
if burned slowly for many hours produces a saleable crude iodine, but it
is wasteful of fuel, and time consuming. The four horses still on Tory
are probably a hangover from the kelp-burning days; they were used
to pull the heavy slide-carts that brought the kelp from the shore to the
kilns. (Donkeys are used for ploughing.) Whatever the reason the turf
is practically gone. Bogs have been allocated to the islanders on the
mainland, but the trouble and expense of exploiting these make it not
worthwhile and the islanders either buy turf and ship it over, or soak
sods in paraffin and burn those. The few remaining bits of good bogland
are highly prized.

The owning of land has now more of a symbolic than a utilitarian
value, although people with cattle and poultry find it useful for growing
animal food. Most people have some potatoes. Other economic activities which have now declined include shore gathering, and spinning and
weaving. The shore was meticulously divided into lots like the land.
The 'king' of the island—an office which has now lapsed—was in fact
the arbiter of shore disputes, and used to apportion the shore divisions
in a lottery. Winkles, edible seaweed, and valuable driftwood were the
main crops. At one time all the women spun their own wool, but this
is now almost a dead art. Some calves are sold to mainland farmers, but
shipping them is very difficult.

At present the shops dominate the economy. They provide credit
over the winter for those remaining on the island, and this is paid off by
the migrants in the summer. Until recently they accepted barter in the
form of fish for salting, but this has now stopped. Shops have been on
the island since just before World War I, but only recently have they
become a source of high profit. The prices are high but the islanders
prefer to pay high prices rather than ship the goods themselves. This
shop-dominated internal economy is something quite new. A few
tourists and birdwatchers also bring in a little money in the summer.
The lighthouse, the post-office, and public works provide a little
employment, and the children gather sea-rod—a kind of seaweed
which is dried and sold for nylon manufacture.

The economy changed from one in which land was intensively used and fishing only supplementary, to one in which fishing dominated and land use became less intensive. This in turn has been replaced by an economy in which the export of labour is the primary source of income, with fishing second and land practically useless. Each of these moves has brought Tory more and more into contact with the outside world, more dependent on it, and more integrated with it.

SOCIAL STRUCTURE

Several facts in the previous sections have pointed to developments and changes in the structure of social relationships. The isolation and relative autonomy of the island have allowed it to develop free from the pressures which have operated on the mainland and have made for a unique social structure. For almost a hundred years now Tory has been free from landlord control, and for that matter from almost any control. Local authorities and central governments have found it impossible to exert much authority over the island. Taxes and rates are not collected, licences are rarely obtained, land laws virtually unknown. The island goes its own way.[1] But gradually, it has been forced into closer association with the wider world. The Congested Districts Board first, and then the County Council (after 1898) and various, ministries (after 1922) began to invest in the island. A substructure of roads, slipways, harbours, winches, etc. laid the basis for an expanding economy. A nurse and a post-office were introduced. Priest, nurse, postmistress, and lighthouse-keepers came to form a small elite, which has now been supplemented by the more prosperous of the shopkeepers. Improved communications have meant that contacts with emigrants are maintained and there is a good deal of visiting back and forth, especially between Tory and Scotland.

Various influxes of people from the mainland have added new blood to the island. The traditional families, deriving from ancient times, are the Duggans (Ó Dubhgáin), the Doohans (Ó Dubhghain), the Rogers (Mac Ruadhraigh), and possibly the Divers (Ó Duibhir). These still account for the majority of the islanders. Table V shows how these have been supplemented by other surnames.[2] The origin of some of the more

---

[1] The rating valuation records for 1864 have a note which mentions a police barracks at an annual rent of £12. Joule's pamphlet mentions that the county cess collector was saved from murder in 1871 by four policemen 'temporarily stationed in Tory in consequence of Fenian designs'. Clearly police have never been a fixture on the island, and the valuation records have no entry for a barracks after 1871. British soldiers were stationed on the island in World War I, but this was for defence purposes.

[2] Those for 1830–40 were taken from the Tithe Aplottment Roll, (Public Records Office, Dublin); those for 1857 from the *General Valuation of Rateable Property in Ireland* (Richard Griffiths, Commissioner; Dublin 1857), volume on

ancient of these is still known. The Whoriskeys (Ó Fuaruisce) are traced back to two cousins, Tomás Dubh and Domhnall-Shiubhainne, who were shipwrecked on the island at the end of the eighteenth century, and who remained to marry island girls and settle down. The two branches still maintain their separate identity and trace their genealogies back over six or seven generations. Most of the others are known to have married into the island. Some—those in brackets—were transitory and left neither memory nor issue. Ward, who married into the island in the late nineteenth century, was the entrepreneur responsible for starting the hotel.

TABLE V. Tory Surnames from ancient times to 1964

pre-1750	1830–40	1857	1903	1964
Rogers	+	+	+	+
Duggan	+	+	+	+
Doohan	+	+	+	+
Diver	+	+	+	+
	Meenan	+	+	+
	McClafferty	+	+	+
	Whoriskey	+	+	+
	McGinley	+	+	+
	Herraghty	+	+	−
	Curran	+	+	−
	(Coyle)	−	−	−
	(McElroy)	−	−	−
		(Minnion)	−	−
		Mooney	+	−
			Ward	−
			O'Donnel	+
			Dixon	+
			Doherty	+
			Carrol	+
			O'Brien	−
			Gallagher	−
				McGinty
				Boyle
				McGonagle
				Burke
				Hendron

Note: Names, appearing on various lists, that are known to have belonged to people who did not marry in Tory, such as casual labourers, etc., are excluded. 'Minnion' (see 1857 list) *could* be a misrendering of 'Meenan'. Those persons whose names appear in brackets were transitory and left no issue.

Despite this influx, however, the island was relatively endogamous. A number of dispensations have been granted over the last forty years

the Union of Dunfanaghy; those for 1903 from the records of the Congested Districts Board (Land Commission); those for 1964 from the author's fieldnotes.

(the only years for which marriage records are available); 12 per cent of the marriages were within the prohibited degree of second cousinship. Both the increase in in-marriages and the recent practice of adopting mainland orphans have widened marriage choice. Even so, the kinship network is complicated and it is commonly said that everyone can trace some relationship to everyone else. From this network, however, various groupings emerge. One of the more interesting, although functionally one of the least effective, is the 'clan'. 'Clann' in Gaelic means 'children' or 'descendants' of a person, and it is common on Tory to identify certain groups of people as, for example, 'clann Eóghain'—the descendants of Eóghan (Owen), or something such. A group of this kind will consist of *all* the descendants of the eponymous ancestor, often over as many as eight or more generations, although the average depth is six. The continuity of the group is reflected in the naming system. For example, the founder of such a group, one Nellie Doohan, had three children; Mary-Nellie, Liam-Nellie, and Eóghan-Nellie. Their children were Seán-Mary-Nellie, Caitlín-Liaim-Nellie, John-Eóghain-Nellie etc. The children of the latter were John-John-Eóghain-Nellie and Nábla-John-Eóghain and so on down the generations. The relative strength of the groups can almost be judged from the continuity of the names (Fox, 1963). I say 'relative strength' because clearly the clans competed with each other for allegiance of members. A man was a member of as many 'clans' as he had known lineal ancestors who were members, but of course he could not always keep up multiple allegiances. The functions of these groups are obscure and they are probably to some extent a historical hangover from the days when genealogy was more important. They seem to arise from persons of importance who held the allegiance of their children, grandchildren, etc. unto the nth generation. If such a person had land, then it would be in the interests of his or her descendants to maintain contact in the event of inheritance. If, for example, a man inherited land from his mother and died without heirs, then the land must revert through his mother, i.e. to someone of one of her 'clans'. Apart from this, pride in genealogy and a vague sense of obligation ('you can't deny them') holds together people with a 'clan-founding' common ancestor. Smaller segments of such clans—the children of, say, a common great-grandparent—were often very close, exchanging mutual services and supporting each other in feuds.

This latter point is important, because, although Tory presented a united front to the outside world, it was, like all such communities, torn periodically by internecine strife. This generally flared up between individuals, but tended to involve the kin of each in varying degrees. Land, boats, and women were the commonest sources of quarrels. On the latter point rests what is perhaps the most significant and unique of Tory institutions. This was the connection between marriage and household. The Tory ideal of the family, rooted in religion and in custom, is that its bonds are unbreakable. The loyalties between parents and children and between siblings override all others. But this of course contains a paradox, because in order to form this ideal unit, one has to break up other such ideal units. To found a new family two people have to be torn away from their natal families. This paradox exists elsewhere in Ireland and results in either non-marriage, or in elaborate arrangements for the safeguarding of all parties involved in the family transition at marriage, with dowries and settlements and provisions for the old ones (Arensberg and Kimball, 1940). Now on Tory, although marriage is treason and some people even creep to church at night to get married rather than face the ire of parents and siblings, a compromise is reached. Because the spouses will never be more than walking distance from each other anyway, even after marriage they do not leave their natal homes. The husband stays with his siblings and parents (if they are still alive) and so does the wife. He contributes to her upkeep and perhaps helps to farm her land if she has any, and has 'visiting' rights in her home. Any children stay with their mother. Some of these marriages virtually lapse with the passage of time, but in others the partners are loyal and devoted to each other. Thus a compromise between the duties to aged parents and siblings and those to spouse is achieved, somewhat at the expense of the marriage bond. If a woman's parents and siblings die or emigrate, then a man may move in with his wife—and more rarely vice versa. Not every married couple lived like this, but I was told that they nearly always *started* thus and found a joint home later. At the turn of the century, according to informants, at least half the marriages followed this pattern. Both the shortage of housing space at the time of highest population, and the fact that a woman would not want to move in with her husband's family if he was away working may have helped to intensify this situation. But clearly the compact nature of the settlements and the endogamy of the island made this solution a convenient one. Whatever the feelings about family loyalty, there was an obvious convenience in leaving households as they were during the early years of a marriage and not disrupting them.

At the moment, this pattern is on the decline. There is less pressure on housing space, and modern values and the opinion of the church do not encourage it. However, approximately 20 per cent of married persons are still living apart. If this is correlated with type of household, then it is seen to be most heavily associated with households headed by *widows*, or formed by two or more adult *siblings*. Households containing a *nuclear* family (parents and children) are associated strongly with residence in the man's house, but again, about 30 per cent of married persons live in the wife's house. Table VI shows the relations between the distribution of household types and types of marital residence in 1963. The 'separate' spouses are not simply old people, but include some newly married couples. The details of the whole cycle of such marriages would take up too much space here, but we can see that the custom, though declining, is still very much in evidence.

TABLE VI. Household and marital residence of 102 married persons
(51 marriages)—1963

| Type of household | Residence of Spouses | | | Total |
	Separate	Wife's house	Husband's house	
Sibling/Widow	16	4	2	22
Nuclear	1	16	34	51
Other	3	10	16	29
Total	20	30	52	102

$\chi_4^2 = 37\cdot2 < \rho = \cdot001$.
Source: Author's fieldnotes.
Note: The difficulties of handling the 'separate residence' category make it necessary to show the distribution of married *persons* by household types rather than *marriages* by household types.

With respect to marriage, however, the effective area of marriage choice for the islanders now stretches to England and Scotland and, as we have seen, marriages away from the island are predominating over endogamous marriages. Women who marry Tory men, with one brief exception, have never moved to Tory, and as the supply of marriageable women on Tory now seems to be running dry, the prospects for future marriages on the island are not good.

One final detail on kinship. In the days of the crewing of large herring boats, kinship was useful in obtaining and holding the large crews. The core of each crew was always a group of kin variously related to the 'manager' of the boat. With the coming of motors this large crew became unnecessary, and now it is a small group of patrilineally related males who tend to run the boats.

Kinship ties have not tended to lessen with the passage of time and wider involvement. When young people go abroad to work, they are fed along an extended kinship network through Northern Ireland and Scotland and eventually find hospitality and a job with a kinsman resident there. It is the different use to which these ties are put—migrant labouring—that is important. On the island itself, they are of less and less use, except for mutual support. And here is another Tory paradox. The strength of the old kinship ties is in fact undermining the survival of the island by making migration easier. Because he has an enclave of kin in, say, Glasgow (itself embedded in an enclave of Tory folk), the young migrant finds the same support and familiarity there as he did on the island, and is more likely to stay. Tory boys and girls have now taken to marrying each other in Scotland and staying there.

CONCLUSIONS

From being an island pretty much turned in upon itself, Tory has gradually come to be more and more involved in the affairs of the world. It could not now survive, with its ageing population, unless there were government subsidies and migrant earnings, and both these things push Tory into a relationship with the bureaucratic outside world. From a system of intense face-to-face relationships in which problems had to be solved in customary terms with the help of kin, Tory has moved into a system of involvement in a wider and more impersonal network. Dependence has shifted from the kinship group to various agencies, and outside forces of law and authority can be invoked in disputes. For example, a legal will can be drawn up in favour of one child despite customary practices of equal inheritance. But the very impersonality of the outside world makes 'home' attractive, and most young people, at least at the beginning of their migrating career, want to come back as often as possible. The 'lobster/labouring' complex works well enough for the men, but female migration is a serious threat to island survival.

It has been common, since the first World War, for girls to work away, often for years at a time, and many settled down and married outside. However, enough girls stayed at home to provide marriage partners for the men who, after their intensive period of migrating, wanted to settle down and marry. Of late, however, the majority of young girls have been following the migratory pattern. In 1962 all the marriageable girls left for 'winter' jobs. Girls' migrations are usually of longer duration than the casual work of the men. The young men still average three to four months a year on the island—the girls three to four weeks. The chances of their ever marrying on the island are thought to be slim. Tory is no longer a base for expeditions to the outside world, but a childhood home to return to in the holidays.

For the present generation of schoolchildren the future pattern of life is established. With very few exceptions they will go away to work. This is a conscious ambition with most of them. Only the inadequate will stay. 'Working away' has become a part of the life-cycle, a *rite de passage*, as firmly established as baptism and confirmation. It is the initiation into adulthood.

All this erodes the traditionally strong authority of the old. The young are now the breadwinners. They know that they will leave sooner or later and so the sanctions of the old have less force. Loyalty to parents is fierce and contributions to their upkeep large, but obedience to their stricter tenets, for example over marriage choice, is not so automatic as it might have been. Indeed the old rarely try to exert authority. They have become dependent, and the young are the adaptable and successful.

The old people are ambivalent about migration. They feel that the young should migrate to earn money, but at the same time they want to keep them at home. If anything, fathers are keenest for their sons to migrate, and mothers most anxious to retain them. No one wants the girls to go, but they are resigned to this exodus. The feeling is that 'there is nothing here for them'. But again the situation is paradoxical. A son who does not stay at home is disloyal, but one who does not go away to work is lazy.

There could be opportunity for some enterprise in the sphere of boatbuilding in which fathers and sons might join. The Tory men are skilled boatbuilders and the boats they build for themselves are greatly admired. However, most of the likely candidates are relatively permanent islanders who receive the 'dole' (unemployment compensation) and this has come to be regarded as a regular subsidy. Any kind of profitable self-employment would mean the end of this subsidy and this is greatly feared. Wives in particular put pressure on their husbands not to 'lose the dole'.[1] They prefer this small but reliable income to the uncertain prospect of high profits from industry. In a sense, the certainty of unemployment benefit inhibits risk taking, and so perpetuates unemployment. (This is not unique to Tory but is a problem all over the west of Ireland.)

The exceptions to this rule are the shopkeepers. One of these shows tremendous enterprise and has even installed an electric generator, running wires to several West Town houses at a monthly charge. He shipped over a van and runs goods to the East Town. He has installed in his house the first bathroom on the island (outside the parochial house). Another shopkeeper has brought over a tractor which he hires out for ploughing and hauling, and, more importantly, uses in contract work for the lighthouse and the county council. This man has a boat which is engaged in year-round fishing with a largely non-Tory crew. The shopkeepers differ with regard to their estimates of future

[1] Wives in the 'separate' marriages described earlier receive by customary right half the husband's dole.

prospects. The one with the generator and bathroom looks forward to a prosperous future. The others seem to see their strategy as making and saving as much as possible against the prospect of pulling out. They do not seem to specialize and each shop is more or less a duplicate of the others. Their great problem, as with all peasant shopkeepers, is the juggling of credit. They see themselves as being at the mercy of the islanders as they have no sanctions against bad debtors. Needless to say, the islanders do not see it this way. But such is the state of affairs on the island now, with the decline of land use and fishing and the change in notions of an adequate standard of living, that people are utterly dependent on the shops and the shops are locked into a complex of credit relationships with the people. This dominance of the shopkeeper and the nature of the relationships with him is a real shift in the Tory system of role-relationships, and one to which adjustment is difficult.

I have not dealt with changes on the cultural side, but it is here that the decline of the old way of life is most obvious. Although, for example, every Tory islander speaks Gaelic as his first language, years of working away and recent intensification of contacts with Britain have made most of them bi-lingual. As very few of them are effectively literate in Gaelic, the only way they increase their vocabularies is through English, so that even their Gaelic has a heavy English content. They listen mostly to English programmes on the wireless. Most important of all, all the migrants write home in English. The old songs, prayers, proverbs, and stories are known to a declining few.

At the root of all this is migration. Without migration they could not survive, yet migration is gradually eroding their way of life and robbing them of their young. We have come a long way from the problems of sheer physical survival. The problem is no longer how to live with the sea and with each other and not starve. The problem now is to persuade young people to stay and make their homes on the island. But this is impossible for many reasons, and Tory can probably only look forward to a further decline. With a predominantly aged population depending more and more on subsidies, and growing lonelier and lonelier in the winters, it is perhaps only a matter of time before the government evacuates the island.

10

LEGISLATIVE-EXECUTIVE RELATIONS IN SMALLER TERRITORIES

A. W. Singham

ONE of the most difficult problems that confronts many of the new members of the Commonwealth is the question of defining legislative-executive relations (Subramaniam, 1962). This problem, however, is not confined to these newly independent countries, for we find that even in many older countries this problem has not been successfully resolved (Chubb, 1963). However, for our particular purposes we are interested primarily in the relationship between the civil servant and the elected ministers in several small societies in the British West Indies. In small societies we are able to collect and possibly comprehend various types of data which may not be possible in larger and more complex societies. Further, small societies have certain unique characteristics which require separate analytical treatment. Hence, we will observe, as in this paper, the inappropriateness of institutions and methods of analysis that have been devised for larger and more complex societies. In this particular context we shall examine the problems created by the establishment of ministerial systems of government in small societies, indicating the difficulties and problems that emerge between the legislative and executive branches of government. We will begin by discussing the constitutional and legal requirements of office and then observe how these requirements have been interpreted by the participants in several territories. In the course of the analysis a number of theoretical propositions that have been recently advanced about bureaucracy and political development will be examined wherever relevant.[1] We shall resist the temptation, however, either to use or evolve 'models' to explain change in the British Caribbean, rather confining ourselves to the evidence and wherever appropriate making the relevant connection between theory and practice.

[1] Cf. F. Riggs, 1962: 'An Ecological Approach: The "Sala" Model', in Heady, F. and Stokes, S. (ed.), *Papers in Comparative Public Administration*, Institute of Public Administration, University of Michigan, Ann Arbor, Michigan; and Shils, E., 1963: 'Demagogues and Cadres in the Political Development of the New States', in Pye, L. W. (ed.), *Communications and Political Development*, Princeton, N.J.; also La Palombara, J. (ed.), 1963: *Bureaucracy and Political Development*, Princeton, N.J.

Martin Wight maintains that there are two principles of subordination in Crown Colony government (Wight, 1952). The first is that the legislature is subordinate to the executive; the second is that the colonial government is subordinate to the imperial government. In the West Indies there has been a gradual movement from Crown Colony status to internal self-government and in some cases to independence. However, constitutional development has been uneven, with Barbados and Jamaica holding somewhat unique positions. Even within the Windward and Leeward groups there have been some variations in the types of constitutions. In this paper, after assessing the general problems in the area briefly, we shall examine two territories, Grenada and British Guiana, in more detail.

During the early fifties a number of West Indian territories made considerable advances towards self-government. In June 1950 the Windward group was offered a new type of constitution, the most significant feature being the introduction of universal adult suffrage. In each territory the legislature was to consist of fourteen members, eight of whom were to be elected by popular vote. The remainder were to be made up of the Administrator as President, the Financial Secretary, the Attorney General, and three nominees of the Governor of the Windwards. The eight elected members were then to elect three of their number to the Executive Council, which was, however, still to be dominated by the official members. The Leewards were offered similar constitutions, and elections were held in all territories late in 1951. Throughout the area new types of political organizations emerged, with labour or labour orientated candidates tending to predominate in the legislatures. In British Guiana the Waddington Constitution was put into effect in 1953, and in the election which followed the People's Progressive Party led by Dr Jagan gained control of the Legislative Council.

Political parties began to emerge, in some cases as adjuncts of the trade unions. What is significant about these elections is that for the first time members of the labouring classes made their presence known directly in the political system. There was a tendency to move away from middle class leaders and more politicians began to come from the lower classes, including agricultural workers and small farmers.

The political order was seriously transformed by the emergence of this class on to the political scene. Colonial officials now faced the problem of working with these new leaders. In many instances they were openly contemptuous of these 'upstart' politicians. On the other hand the politicians were so impressed by the titles and the rituals of office that they assumed that the new constitution gave them absolute executive power. However, the executive was still dominated by officials, and the Legislative Council was devised primarily to co-opt these new elites into the political system.

These new constitutions were in effect to provide a period of tutelage for self-government. In accordance with this objective a number of territories adopted in 1954 the Committee system whereby the elected members were given some executive responsibilities. This gave way to a ministerial system in the Leewards in 1956 and the Windwards in 1959. The latter change took place, however, within the context of a broader West Indian Federation, the objective being that all the unit territories were to have similar constitutional structures irrespective of size. Furthermore, there was increasing pressure from the Legislative Councils for a greater share of executive responsibility. During this whole period there were increasing tensions between the executive and legislative branches. The pattern of adjustment depended greatly on the type of politician in each territory and the Governor or Administrator. In Jamaica, for example, Sir Hugh Foot openly announced that he was planning his own obsolescence from the political arena. Foot was fortunate, however, in that his legislative counterpart, Alexander Busta-mante, was a shrewd politician who did not openly challenge the executive authority, but concentrated on exercising authority in the legislative arena and delegated responsibility to the civil service. In the two territories of Grenada and British Guiana, however, a harmonious pattern did not emerge. There the tensions between the civil service and the legislature led to open conflict and eventually resulted in both these territories having their constitutions suspended.

The evolution of the ministerial system in the Caribbean resulted from the London Conference of 1956, when the various West Indian territories, with the exception of British Guiana, agreed to the creation of a federation. Fiscal control over the grant-aided territories was to be transferred from the Colonial Office to the Federal Government (Grenada, Council Paper No. 1, 1956). Gradually the executive powers of the Administrators or Governors were to be transferred to the Chief Ministers, who in the smaller territories were also to hold the portfolio of finance. In addition there were also to be three other ministers and a minister without portfolio. The Administrator, however, was to retain control over the judiciary, police, and the public service. Under this system the Administrator normally asked the Leader of the majority party in the Legislature to form the government, and with the advice of the Chief Minister appointed the other ministers. Each minister was responsible for a number of departments under his portfolio; in addition he was assigned a principal secretary who was administratively responsible for the activities of all the Departments under his Ministry.

This type of constitution gave the territories semi-responsible government and under normal circumstances the next step in constitutional evolution has been internal self-government. It should be stressed, however, that the territories we are dealing with are quite small and the economists have pointed out that the governmental structure is somewhat elaborate for these territories (Lewis, 1962; Morgan, Appendix, p. 149). Lewis provides some suggestive data in this regard: using Trinidad as a base, he devises an excess burden per cent for various territories in the West Indies, which he measures by dividing his index of civil service pay by the index of national income per head and subtracting unity.

	Civil Service Pay Index	National Income per head	Excess Burden per cent
Trinidad	100	100	0
Barbados	72	48	50
Windwards	60	30	100
Leewards	65	36	81

Source: W. A. Lewis, 'Eastern Caribbean Federation', p. 20.

The cost of administration is particularly relevant because some of the territories involved are dependent on grants to meet their operating costs. Perhaps a more important drawback of a ministerial system for small territories than expenditure is that it encourages separateness and makes manifest their latent parochial tendencies. In other words the elaborate constitutional structure makes it psychologically and practically difficult for these territories to move towards regional collaboration. It could be argued that this indeed was one of the major stumbling blocks of the short-lived West Indian Federation.

This type of constitution has also encouraged the growth of a party system in each individual territory. The Administrator, for example, called on the person most capable of gaining majority support in the Legislative Council to be Chief Minister and on his advice appointed the rest of the 'cabinet'. This eventually led to a party system, and since the area of policy disagreements was small it encouraged a party system of 'in' and 'out' parties. In a sense this had the same effect as introducing party competition into local government. In addition, it has been found that in many new countries there is a tremendous shortage of persons willing and qualified to participate in public life. This shortage becomes all the more important in smaller territories where the skills of the members of the 'out' party are not employed. The partisanship that is engendered is not only wasteful of skills already in short supply, but is dysfunctional in other respects as well. Partisanship nurtures and encourages factionalism in the society at large, and while larger societies are often able to vitiate the effects of political partisanship, smaller societies find it difficult to do so. The end result is that parties reward their friends and punish their enemies. In small underdeveloped societies where government is usually the major employer, the effects of this are widespread, and a great deal of insecurity results, particularly when there is a change of government. This further encourages the parties and their followers when in power to accumulate enough wealth to maintain themselves when out of power.

We can summarize the situation as follows. The political system in smaller territories encourages and nurtures particularism, which is exactly the reverse of the intention of the framers of their constitutions, who had rather hoped that this type of constitutional order would encourage universalism. This is not surprising since the framers were influenced by their own experiences as members of large industrial societies with a constitutional system evolved over a long period. They were not particularly concerned or conversant with the peculiarities of small agricultural societies.

The most serious consequence of partisanship, however, has been its dramatic effect on legislative-executive relations. The civil servant is placed in a very awkward position in a small and highly partisan political atmosphere. The political executive demands loyalty and loyalty in this case means partisan loyalty. If he does become partisan, however, he takes an enormous risk, for if his party loses at the next election he is likely to be penalized. Even if he displays normal administrative loyalty he is always suspect during the first few months of the new government. Furthermore the smallness of the society makes anonymity a myth, and administrative matters are often publicly discussed, thus making administrative secrecy difficult. The civil servant is apt to try and meet this difficult situation by becoming what the Jamaicans call a member of the P.I.P. (Party in Power). A P.I.P. civil servant, however, is not likely to enjoy the confidence of the ministers, and he normally is not sought after for advice. The second alternative is for him to become administratively over-cautious which does not encourage the imagination which is required for implementing government programmes. The technical branch of the service is also affected by the partisan atmosphere. Although the technician is by temperament normally non-partisan, he finds that his administrative counterpart enjoys more status and power. Further, in order to get support for his programmes he often feels it necessary to bypass the administrators and gain direct access to the minister. This often results in his becoming a civil service 'politician', thus diverting him from his technical functions. This process often tends to make the more junior technicians cynical and encourages young persons to aim for administrative rather than technical careers. The resulting dearth of technicians creates often insurmountable difficulties in planning and implementing programmes of economic development.

One final point deserves our attention before turning to our two case studies. The senior and middle levels of the civil service in smaller territories tend to form the bulk of the urban middle class. They are normally the most articulate and powerful of the elite groups in the community. The political executive in some territories, however, comes from the labouring or peasant class. Hence class position seriously affects the attitudes of these two groups to one another. Furthermore, the civil servant is normally located in the capital and tends to be contemptuous of the rural origins of the politician. The politician similarly often reflects the rural hostility to the urban values of the civil servant.

If these tensions become acute, a pattern of legislative-executive relations evolves that might dramatically be described as one of terror and sabotage. The politician terrorizes the civil servant in the market place, sometimes referring to him by name and threatening his future. The civil servant retaliates by sabotaging the minister; in one extreme case by refusing to let his minister have some files on the grounds that they had been declared secret and confidential. Terror and sabotage are extreme terms, but in small societies where jobs are scarce politics are taken very seriously, and these relationships seriously affect all other social relations in the community.

GRENADA

The island of Grenada belongs to the Windward group and its constitutional evolution has been similar to the other Windward and the Leeward islands. While her political connections were with the Windwards, her people have had long associations with Trinidad, and it is estimated that approximately 30,000 Grenadians live in Trinidad. There is considerable movement of people between Trinidad and Grenada.

In 1960 the population of Grenada was 88,677 people, who live in an area of 133 square smiles. The majority of the population is African in origin; while close on two-thirds are Roman Catholic, the rest belong to a variety of Protestant denominations. Over 87 per cent of the farms are 5 acres or less; however, 50 per cent of total farm acreage belongs to estates of 100 acres and over in size. About 90 per cent of the country's exports are derived from three major crops: cocoa, nutmegs and mace, and bananas. In the 1950s there was considerable migration to Great Britain, and in 1960 alone as many as 3,400 left for Great Britain, which represents 3·8 per cent of the total population. Grenada is smaller in size than the smallest Jamaican parish, or approximately the size of the Isle of Wight. In 1959 Grenada was granted a ministerial form of government with a constitution similar to the Jamaican constitution of 1944.

In 1951 Grenada faced a severe social and economic crisis (M. G. Smith, 1961). In the same year she was also granted universal adult franchise and a new constitution. It also marked the beginning of the political career of E. M. Gairy, a 21-year-old ex-school teacher, son of a small farmer, who led a successful strike in February 1951. Gairy had just returned from the Dutch island of Aruba and had spent some time there as a labour union organizer.

Gairy dominated Grenadian politics throughout the fifties. He was elected to the Legislative Council in 1951 and 1954, lost his franchise in 1957, but won again in 1961 and 1962. In 1961 his party, the GULP, won 8 of the 10 seats, and the Administrator asked him, after his franchise had been restored, to be the Chief Minister of Grenada. In June of 1961 the Administrator, acting on the findings of a Commission of Enquiry, suspended the constitution and relieved Mr Gairy and his associates of their respective portfolios. We shall recount the major events that led to this suspension which reveal some of the tensions that arose between the civil service and the political executive in Grenada (Singham, 1964). It will be recalled that the constitution of 1959 introduced a ministerial system, with the Administrator retaining some of his executive powers.

One major problem was that the Administrator was accountable to three bodies: the Secretary of State for the Colonies, the Legislature of Grenada, and the Federal Minister of Finance. The Federal Government was represented in Grenada at that time by a Federal Economic Adviser. He had no official position in the colony's administration, but enjoyed considerable informal power. Since Grenada was a grant-aided territory, he advised the Federal Government on all fiscal matters relating to Grenada.

Ultimately, however, the Administrator was, in the words of the famous Colonial Regulation 105, 'the single and supreme authority responsible to and representative of Her Majesty'. The constitution recognized the fact that the Administrator would have to act generally with the advice of the Executive Council, but he could disregard their advice if the matter required urgent attention or was so insignificant that it did not require consultation.

In addition to having the usual reserve powers, the Administrator also was given the power to appoint the members of the Public Service Commission, who in turn were made responsible to him for all disciplinary measures in the public service. The constitution required him to consult with the Chief Minister before making any senior administrative appointments. This became a major area of disagreement between the Administrator and the Chief Minister. Both argued that they had ultimate power and control over the service.

The 1959 Constitution also specified that fiscal control and responsibility was to be shared by the Administrator and the Chief Minister, who is also Minister of Finance. Despite this, the Chief Minister claimed that the Constitution gave him complete fiscal and financial authority. Hence the two major issues dividing the Chief Minister and the Administrator were who was ultimately responsible for the civil service, and fiscal accountability and responsibility.

A further source of tensions arose because Gairy had always displayed his contempt for what he called 'colonial laws'. In fact, he charged that from 1951 on he had always been discriminated against by these laws. In 1952, for example, he refused to have his driver's licence renewed. A court order was issued prohibiting him from driving in Grenada; he retaliated by employing a chauffeur. In 1957 he had more serious trouble with the law when he was convicted of violating an election law and was disenfranchised. Though disenfranchised, he campaigned for his party during the 1961 elections, when, as already noted, his party won 8 out of the 10 seats in the Legislative Council. Soon after the election Gairy claimed that he was *de facto* Chief Minister, and proceeded to announce his cabinet from the market-place. He had little patience with constitutional niceties, and demanded that he be re-enfranchised immediately and formally inducted as Chief Minister. He was eventually granted his franchise later in 1961. During the period between the election and his re-enfranchisement, he proceeded to conduct government from his home and announced public policy from the market square.

The Administrator was in a difficult position. He was not required by law to consult Gairy, but he was fully aware that the majority party in the Legislative Council was loyal only to its leader, Mr Gairy. Speaking in the tradition of the civil service he publicly welcomed the new government and pledged his co-operation. Gairy returned to the House in a jubilant and confident mood. In his opening speech in the Legislative Council he replied with characteristic flamboyance:

In another place, Mr Speaker, I was sworn in as Chief Minister of Grenada, Carriacou and Petit Martinique, and today I am sworn in as a Member of the Legislative Council of this territory. The praises are not due me, but are due the Divine Maker, the Divine Architect, who in His divine scheme of things, saw fit to have me come back to the scene. I am reminded of this divine and equitable law—a law also which lends itself to the maxim that 'cream will always float'. (Grenada, *Leg. Co. Minutes*, December, 1961.)

He went on to point out that the 1959 Constitution depended on a party system and he said, 'I am somewhat, if not totally, responsible for the party system in Grenada'. And finally he concluded his speech by a radical demand for the nationalization of the Sugar Industry. Ten years earlier he was making wage demands as a union leader and now he was using the instrument of the state to frighten the plantocracy.

The office of Chief Minister had in many ways transformed Gairy, but it did not change his style. In his first public speech after assuming office, he said, 'Today I am more the man of action. About four or five years ago, I would have given a long speech but today I give my heart.'

Shortly after assuming office, he took an active interest in the information service, reorganized the Department, and suspended the information officer, replacing him with his own appointee. The *Citizens' Weekly* was renamed the *Star* and its format changed. The *Star* was to become Gairy's answer to the other two newspapers. These papers had been generally hostile to him in the past, and he now had a public opinion organ to reply to his critics. The editor developed a 'newsy' style in reporting, and the paper soon became something more than a government newsletter. The *Star* became the forum for his attacks on the civil service. The *Star* of 16 June 1962 reported the Chief Minister as saying that the civil service must stay clear of politics. As early as December, 1961, however, he had admonished one of his technical officers for his arrogant attitude towards other civil servants.

In September 1961 he held monthly meetings with the heads of departments and the 30 September issue of the *Star* contained the following:

The Chief Minister stressed the point that the Ministers of Government—the elected heads—are the ones in control of the Departments, and not the Administrator.

There must be good relationship between the Heads and the Ministers for it's Ministers they have to please and not the Administrator. That he said is appreciated by the *Colonial Office*. (Emphasis mine.)

One of the major disagreements between the Chief Minister and the Administrator arose as to who had ultimate responsibility for the Service. The Administrator pointed out that he was technically head of the Service, and all matters relating to conditions of work were his responsibility. The virtual dismissal of the information officer was the first case in point. The Chief Minister being a politician depended on political support, and hence wanted to control the information media. Traditionally, however, information services had been the functions of the civil service. The Chief Minister wanted to politicize this bureaucratic agency. The Administrator on his part felt that if the office was to become politicized then proper procedure should be adopted to formalize it. In other words, the Public Service Commission should be consulted in making the post a contractual one. The continued insistence of the Chief Minister that he be responsible for the recruitment and discipline of the Service got him into further difficulties. He inherited, for example, a Financial Secretary who was not well liked by members of the Service. The constitution allowed for Permanent Secretaries to be transferred after consultation between the Chief Minister and the Administrator. The Financial Secretary was, to say the least, not on cordial terms with the Chief Minister, who was also his Minister of Finance. The Financial Secretary was by predisposition an accountant, with a strong predilection for detail. His Minister, as we have seen, was not particularly noted for his love for regulations. Probably the ultimate difficulty was that it was difficult to establish any adequate machinery whereby both the civil servants and the ministers could be prepared for ministerial government. These disagreements resulted in the Chief Minister acting without the advice of his chief technical adviser on financial matters. The Chief Minister depended on his own appointee, his Permanent Secretary, for fiscal matters.

We must remember also that constitutional developments during the period 1959–61 were affected by the movement for independence in the form of the West Indian Federation. The Administrator conceived of himself as a West Indian, presiding over the last stages of the Empire. But by December 1961 with the break-up of the Federation he had to make a dramatic readjustment and become Her Majesty's representative in Grenada. In other words, the attitudes of the politician and civil servants were affected by the expected changes that were to follow after Independence. Gairy reflected this mood of independence in his election campaign in 1961, and the Administrator too talked about the winds of change that were to sweep the colonial world. The tension between the civil service and the political leaders must be viewed then in this changing atmosphere from colonial status to independence and then a return to colonial status again. In other words, the Grenada civil service and its politicians reflected the same anxiety that faced the community at large, namely the anxiety that arose from problems of identity.

The issue that brought the crisis to a head was that of fiscal control. It will be recalled that fiscal responsibility was to be shared by three offices: the Federal Government, the Administrator and the Minister of Finance—Chief Minister in Grenada. Gairy's attitude to economic development and growth was strongly influenced by his early experiences as a trade unionist. He wanted to increase government spending, which would result in greater employment, and most of all he wanted that policy to be identified with himself. He characterized his government as a 'giving' government. This attitude of personalism in economic matters often led him to disregard bureaucratic and technical advice on procedure. His contempt for regulations, especially on questions of government expenditure, led to a popular characterization of his government as suffering from 'squandermania'. Gairy called his spending 'Uncle's way of giving poor people food and jobs'.

The Administrator, however, was not impressed by his spending habits and since the Federation was no longer going to be primarily responsible for financial control over the expenditure of government funds, his responsibility had increased. In the final analysis he would be held responsible to the Secretary of State for the Colonies in regard to Grenada's finances. He then called for an audit on a particular month's expenditure. This report convinced him that there was considerable irregularity and he called for a Commission of Enquiry. Gairy challenged the right of the Administrator to appoint such a Commission but this was overruled by the courts and a thorough investigation was undertaken. The Commission of Enquiry concluded that Gairy had not only been fiscally irresponsible but that in addition had seriously affected the morale and efficiency of the civil service (Grenada, *Commission of Enquiry*, 1962).

Gairy replied with the charge that the Administrator and other senior civil servants had connived to sabotage his government. He went as far as to charge the civil service with being sympathetic to the opposition party. He was personally convinced, however, that he had been working within the confines of the constitution, but the Administrator and the Commission were equally convinced that he had violated the principles of honest government. The findings of the Commission resulted in the suspension of the Constitution on 14 June 1962.

BRITISH GUIANA

British Guiana represents a somewhat different case, but the basic problems are similar. Like other territories in the British Caribbean, a Legislative Council system elected by limited franchise gave way to a Legislative Council elected by universal adult franchise. The major change in Guianese constitutional development occurred in 1953. Like the 1959 Constitution in Grenada the Waddington Constitution provided for a greater degree of self-government. The Waddington Constitution provided for a bicameral legislature: a lower house of 24 members to be elected, and a nominated upper house. The Executive Council was to consist of the Governor as president, three official, ex officio members, i.e. the Chief Secretary, the Financial Secretary and the Attorney-General, and six ministers elected by the lower house.

One of the elected ministers was in turn to be elected Leader of the House. The Governor, however, was to have reserve powers and here again he was gradually to become the titular head of the government. Elections were held on 27 April 1953, with the People's Progressive Party, led by Dr Jagan and supported by Mr Burnham, obtaining 18 of the 24 seats. Dr Jagan was elected Leader of the House, and six members of the P.P.P. held portfolios in the new government. In October 1953, six months after the election, the Governor, using his reserve powers, suspended the constitution and relieved the ministers of their portfolios.

The framers of the Waddington Constitution had anticipated a period of transition during which the Executive Council would be dominated by a council of 'elders'. They had not anticipated the emergence of a highly organized Marxist party with concrete views about government. For example, the Constitution envisaged that only after a suitable period of tutelage would collective responsibility emerge. It was hoped that collective responsibility would emerge as the Executive Council increased its functions. While recognizing the need for increasing responsibility, the Waddington Commission was quick to point out that the powers of ministers should be limited (G.B., Col. No. 280, 1951).

The major difficulties that arose between the ministers and the officials were precisely over the powers and responsibilities of the two branches of government. The officials were jealous of their own responsibilities and privileges. They accused the P.P.P. not only of irresponsibility but of partisanship. The P.P.P. as an organized party assumed that their political power gave them the right to use that power to bring about drastic social and economic reform. In fact they conceived of themselves as a 'people's' government with a moral obligation to usher in the era of socialism. The Waddington Constitution, on the other hand, required instead that the ministers use the opportunity to become acquainted with the machinery of government. It envisaged a period of collaboration and co-operation between the ministers and the civil service. The two groups then not only disagreed about the interpretation of the Constitution but they were in fundamental disagreement about the very nature of civil government (Chase, n.d.; British Guiana, *Suspension of Constitution*, 1953).

The Robertson Commission, appointed after the suspension of the Constitution, reported that the Ministers had deliberately obstructed good government in British Guiana (G.B., Cmd. 9274, 1954). They listed the various instances where ministers had clearly indicated their hostility towards the service. In a number of areas the P.P.P. had little doubt that the Waddington Constitution was full of bourgeois niceties designed to hoodwink the masses.

Officially the Constitution was suspended on the grounds that mis-management by the P.P.P. was leading to violence.[1] In British Guiana the conflict was complicated by the fact that the political party involved was anti-civil service not only because of the struggle for legislative supremacy over the executive, but also in terms of ideology.

CONCLUSIONS

These two cases are quite suggestive in regard to the nature of legislative-executive relations in territories which have constitutions providing for limited self-government. Both constitutions required that the participants share similar values about government. It is quite apparent that in Grenada and British Guiana the legislative leaders and the executive officials did not share the same values. Differences in values, however, do not fully explain why conflict arose. We have seen that the constitutions themselves on occasion gave rise to misunder-standings. The framers of the constitutions in both cases were following British practice by making rigid distinctions between policy and ad-ministration. This naïve view of the separation of powers has been seriously questioned in other contexts (Chapman, 1959). One of the consequences of this point of view is that it leads some observers to conclude that the major distinction is that while colonial administration is primarily concerned with the maintenance of law and order national administration is concerned primarily with welfare (Eisenstadt, 1963). This over-simplified view of colonial administration does not take into account the fact that colonial administration, like national administra-tion, has had to distribute welfare in order to remain in power. British colonial administration has been noted for its capacity to deal with local interests and involve them through the machinery of Legislative Councils and to exercise influence without relying primarily on violence. It is quite clear that colonial administrators have used both formal and informal machinery to distribute welfare and hence main-tain themselves in power.

With a heritage of involvement in the policy-making process the colonial civil servant often finds it difficult to come to any working relationship with the elected politician, especially during the period of transfer of power from Crown Colony status to more responsible government. There tends to develop a power struggle between these two holders of office, and the political style may become one of terror and sabotage. The politician who is sensitive about his newly acquired

[1] In another context I attempt to show that the real reason for the suspension was not domestic issues but rather international ones. Cf. my 'Race, Class and Ideology in British Guiana', University of Manchester, December 1963, forth-coming.

power views advice sceptically while, on the other hand, the civil servant is apt to be quite hostile to what appear to him as novel and dramatic policies of the politician. If terror and sabotage become the pattern in the relationship between these two groups, political disorder follows.

It might be useful at this juncture to turn to Max Weber and observe the relevance of his propositions in understanding developments in these two territories (Bendix, 1960). Weber, it will be recalled, distinguished between three types of domination systems: traditional, charismatic and legal. In both Grenada and British Guiana we find that all three of these domination systems co-exist and indeed come into conflict with one another. In Grenada, for example, we could characterize Gairy as a charismatic type fulfilling some of Weber's requirements. To begin with, he emerges at a time of crisis in 1951; he tends also to be revolutionary at this time. He develops two political styles; as a trade union and mass leader he depends upon his personal mission or his charismatic appeal to wield power. At the same time, the electoral system forces him to operate in the world of constitutional politics. When he assumes power in 1961 he finds great difficulty understanding and living by regulations. He proceeds to rule by patronage, or as the Grenadians are fond of saying 'by giving'. His charismatic appeal, however, faced gradual transformation (we prefer to use this term suggested by Bendix rather than routinization) as he continued to participate in constitutional politics. This political movement continued to have a personalist character, even though his party organization showed signs of bureaucratization and routinization. The transformation of his political attitudes is reflected in his response to the question as to whether Crown Colony government provided a good preparation for independence. He saw positive aspects of Crown Colony government and on occasion was quite complimentary about the Colonial Office. He still felt, however, that he had a mission, and his mission was to lead his people from bondage to the promised land. It was possible for him to appeal on this level as he was dealing with a rural and folk people. On the night before the election, he spoke to his people from a boat, and prayers and hymn singing were all part of his campaign. This style ran counter to the legalistic tradition that prevailed in the capital of Grenada, the seat of the bureaucracy.

In British Guiana we find a 'universalistic' social movement attempting to challenge the power of colonial bureaucracy and to establish themselves in power. The challenge was articulated in ideological language: the major issue being that the colonial administration enjoyed a privileged position in the society. In western societies bureaucratization was associated with democracy and egalitarianism. In colonial societies, however, the bureaucracy has been associated with privilege and prestige. The P.P.P., however, began by rejecting the constitution in its entirety. It gradually transformed itself into into a parliamentary party, then succumbed to the demands of particularism in a small multi-racial society by becoming a communal party. The P.P.P. however was aided in the latter process by the international political system.

Small societies, then, present real difficulties in the development of harmonious relations between the political executive and the civil service. We find that Dr Benedict's (*supra*, pp. 48–50) notion of universalistic role-relationship has special relevance for our problem. The constitutional order has required that the participants be committed to some universalistic values. On the other hand the society stresses particularism. One solution suggested by Dr Benedict is that tensions could be reduced by having pure democracy. The market-place, however, is a difficult place to conduct government in the West Indies. The rising revolution of expectations in the area would make market-place democracy all the more difficult. The obvious solution, however, lies in greater regional collaboration. The failure of the recent West Indian Federation should not deter the search for new forms of regional collaboration and government in the area. Needless to say, an area that deserves serious attention in this connection, which has been overlooked thus far, is that of strengthening local government while at the same time allowing for federalism.

APPENDIX

Complete List of Papers presented at the Seminar

The Smaller Territories: The External Political Factors *by D. P. J. Wood*
Some Economic Problems of Small Countries *by A. D. Knox* ✓
Sociological Aspects of Smallness *by B. Benedict* ✓
Demographic Aspects of Smallness *by T. E. Smith* ✓
The West Indies *by D. J. Morgan* —
Montserrat: Autonomy in Microcosm *by D. Lowenthal* —
Case Study: British Honduras *by D. A. G. Waddell* ✓
The Grand Duchy of Luxembourg *by K. C. Edwards* ✓
Zanzibar *by W. J. Dourado* —
The Consequences of Smallness in Polynesia *by R. G. Ward* ✓
The Virgin Islands: A Case Study in Smallness *by N. Harrigan* —
The New Hebrides *by J. S. G. Wilson* —
Papua and New Guinea as a Small Territory *by B. B. Schaffer* —
The Cocos Islands *by T. E. Smith* —
The High Commission Territories with Special Reference to Swaziland *by* ✓
    J. E. Spence
Tory Island *by J. R. Fox* ✓
Arab Unity *by E. Kedourie* —
Legislative-Executive Relations in Smaller Territories *by A. W. Singham* ✓
Hong Kong as a Small Territory: Some Aspects of its Economic Development
    by D. J. Dwyer —
Basutoland *by S. Wallman* —
Political Aspects of Smallness: A Summing Up *by D. P. J. Wood* ✓

BIBLIOGRAPHY

ARDENER, E., 1962: 'The Political History of Cameroon', *The World Today*, vol. xviii, no. 8, London.

ARENSBURG, C. M. and KIMBALL, S. T., 1940: *Family and Community in Ireland*, Cambridge, Mass.

BAIN, J. S., 1956: *Barriers to New Competition*, Cambridge, Mass.

BANTON, M. (ed.), 1960: *The Social Anthropology of Complex Societies*, London.

BELSHAW, H., 1960: 'Some Pacific Islands Problems', *Pacific Viewpoint*, vol. I, no. 2, Wellington, N.Z.

BENEDICT, B., 1964: 'Capital, Saving and Credit among Mauritian Indians', in Firth and Yamey (eds.), *Capital, Saving and Credit in Peasant Societies*, London.

BENDIX, R., 1960: *Max Weber, An Intellectual Portrait*, New York.

BLOOD, Sir HILARY, 1958: *The Smaller Territories*, London.

BOHANNAN, P., 1957: *Justice and Judgement among the Tiv*, London.

BORRIE, W. D., FIRTH, R., and SPILLIUS, J., 1957: 'The Population of Tikopia, 1929 and 1952', *Population Studies*, vol. X, Part 3, London.

BOTT, E., 1957: *Family and Social Network*, London.

BRITISH GUIANA, n.d.: *The Constitution, Suspension Ordered on October 8, 1953*, reprinted by Command, The Bureau of Public Information, Georgetown.

CHAPMAN, B., 1959: *The Profession of Government*, London.

CHASE, A., n.d.: *113 Days towards Freedom in Guiana*, Georgetown.

CHUBB, B., 1963: 'Going about Persecuting Civil Servants—The Role of the Irish Parliamentary Representative', *Political Studies*, vol. XI, no. 3, Oxford.

COLE, M., 1961: *South Africa*, London.

DOWNIE, J., 1959: *An Economic Policy for British Honduras*, Belize.

DURKHEIM, E., 1947: *The Division of Labour in Society*, Glencoe, Illinois.

EISENSTADT, S. N., 1956: *From Generation to Generation*, London.

EISENSTADT, S. N., 1963: 'Bureaucracy and Political Development' in J. LaPalombara (ed.), *Bureaucracy and Political Development*, Princeton, N.J.

EVANS-PRITCHARD, E. E., 1951: *Social Anthropology*, London.

F.A.O., 1961: *Production Yearbook 1960*, vol. XIV, Rome.

FERNS, H. S., 1960: *Britain and Argentina in the Nineteenth Century*, London.

FIRTH, R., 1951: *Elements of Social Organisation*, London.

FIRTH, R., 1959: *Social Change in Tikopia*, London.

FIRTH, R. et al., 1957: 'Factions in Indian and Overseas Indian Societies', *British Journal of Sociology*, vol. VIII, London.

FIRTH, R. and YAMEY B. S. (eds.), 1964: *Capital, Saving and Credit in Peasant Societies*, London.

FOSBERG, F. R. (ed.), 1963: *Man's Place in the Island Ecosystem*, Honolulu.

FOX, J. R., 1963: 'Structure of Personal Names on Tory Island', *Man*, vol. LXIII, Article 192, London.

FOX, J. R., 1966: 'Kinship and Land Tenure on Tory Island', *Ulster Folklife*, vol. XII, Belfast.

GREAT BRITAIN, 1943–5: Admiralty Naval Intelligence Division, *Pacific Islands*, 4 vols., London.

GREAT BRITAIN, 1948: Cmd. 7533, *Report of the British Guiana and British Honduras Settlement Commission*, London.

GREAT BRITAIN, 1948: Colonial no. 218, *Conference on the Closer Association of the British West Indian Colonies, held at Montego Bay 1947*, London.

GREAT BRITAIN, 1951: Colonial No. 280, *British Guiana Constitutional Commission 1950–1. Report and Despatch from the Secretary of State for the Colonies*, London.

GREAT BRITAIN, 1954: Cmd. 9274, *Report of the British Guiana Constitutional Commission*, London.

GREAT BRITAIN, 1960: Commonwealth Relations Office, Basutoland, Bechuanaland Protectorate, and Swaziland. *Report of an Economic Survey Mission*, London.

GREAT BRITAIN, 1960: Cmnd. 984, *Report of the British Honduras Conference held in London in February 1960*, London.

GREAT BRITAIN, 1962: *Fiji: Report for the Year 1961*, London.

GREAT BRITAIN, 1962: Cmnd. 1746, *Report of the East Carribbean Federation Conference*, London.

GREAT BRITAIN, 1962: Cmnd. 1814, *The Accession of Aden to the Federation of Southern Arabia*, London.

GREEN, L. P. and FAIR, T. S., 1960: 'Preparing for Swaziland's Economic Growth', *Optima*, vol. 10, no. 4, London.

GREEN, L. P. and FAIR, T. S., 1962: *Development in Africa*, Johannesburg.

GRENADA, 1956: Council Paper No. 1, *Report of the Conference on British Caribbean Federation*, St George's, Grenada.

GRENADA, 1961: Minutes of the Legislative Council.

GRENADA, 1962: *Report of the Commission of Enquiry into the Control of Public Expenditure in Grenada during 1961 and subsequently*, St George's, Grenada.

HENNESSY, W. A. (ed.), 1887: *The Annals of Ulster*, Dublin.

HILL, Lord GEORGE, 1868: *Facts from Gweedore*, 4th Edition, Dublin.

HOMANS, G., 1951: *The Human Group*, London.

JAMAICA, 1962: Department of Statistics, *Quarterly Abstract of Statistics*, March 1962, Kingston.

JAMES, C. L. R., n.d.: *Party Politics in the West Indies*, Trinidad, Vedic Enterprises.

KROEBER, A. L., 1948: *Anthropology*, New York.

KUZNETS, S., 1960: 'Economic Growth of Small Nations', in E. A. G. Robinson (ed.), *The Economic Consequences of the Size of Nations*, London.

LABOUR PARTY, 1957: *Labour's Colonial Policy, Part 3. The Smaller Territories*, London.

LAMBERT, S. M., 1934: 'The Depopulation of Pacific Races', *B. P. Bishop Museum Special Publication 23*, Honolulu.

LAPALOMBARA, J. (ed,). 1963: *Bureaucracy and Political Development*, Princeton, N.J.

LE PAGE, R. B., 1958: 'General Outlines of Creole English Dialects in the British Caribbean', *Orbis*, vol. VII, Louvain.

LEWIS, W. A., 1962: *Eastern Caribbean Federation*, Government of the West Indies, Port of Spain, Trinidad.

MCARTHUR, N., 1961: 'Population and Social Change: The Prospect for Polynesia', *The Journal of the Polynesian Society*, vol. LXX, no. 4, Wellington, N.Z.

MCCOURT, D., 1955: 'The Rundale System in Donegal', *The Donegal Annual*, vol. III, no. 1.

MAC GABHANN, M., 1959: *Rotha Mór an tSaoil*, Dublin.

MAINE, H. S., 1909: *Ancient Law*, London.

MAIR, L. P., 1961: *Safeguards for Democracy*, London.

MAIR, L. P., 1962: *Primitive Government*, London.

MALTA, 1960: Central Office of Statistics: *Demographic Review of the Maltese Islands for the year 1960*, Valletta.

MARQUARD, L., 1961: *The Peoples and Policies of South Africa*, London.

MICKS, W. L., 1925: *History of the Congested Districts Board for Ireland*, Dublin.

NADEL, S. F., 1951: *The Foundations of Social Anthropology*, London.

NEW ZEALAND, 1957, 1962, 1964: Department of Island Territories: *Reports on the Cook, Niue, and Tokelau Islands*, Wellington.

NURKSE, R., 1959: *Patterns of Trade and Development*, Stockholm.

O'DONOVAN, J. (ed.), 1851: *Annala Rioghachta Eireann* (Annals of the Kingdom of Ireland by the Four Masters, from the earliest period to the year 1616), Dublin.

Pacific Islands Monthly: July, September, October, November 1962; July 1964, Sydney.

PARSONS, T., 1937: *The Structure of Social Action*, New York.

PARSONS, T., 1938: 'The Professions and Social Structure', reprinted in *Essays in Sociological Theory, Pure and Applied*, Glencoe, Illinois, 1949.

PARSONS, T., 1951: *The Social System*, Glencoe, Illinois.

PARSONS, T. and SHILS, E., 1951: *Towards a General Theory of Action*, Cambridge, Mass.

PREST, W., 1960: 'A Note on Size of States and Cost of Administration in Australia', in E. A. G. Robinson (ed.), *The Economic Consequences of the Size of Nations*, London.

PROUDFOOT, M. J., 1950: *Population Movements in the Caribbean*, Caribbean Commission, Central Secretariat, Trinidad.

REDFIELD, R., 1955: *The Little Community*, Chicago.

ROBINSON, E. A. G. (ed.), 1960: *The Economic Consequences of the Size of Nations*, London.

SAHLINS, M. D., 1962: *Moala*, Ann Arbor, Michigan.

SCHAPERA, I., 1956: *Government and Politics in Tribal Societies*, London.

SIDEBOTHAM, J. M. 1949: 'The Promontory Fort on Tory Island', *Ulster Journal of Archaeology*, vol. XII, Belfast.

SINGHAM, A. W., 1964: 'Political Process in a Colonial Society', mimeo, unpublished manuscript, Manchester University, forthcoming.

SMITH, M. G., 1961: 'Structure and Crisis in Grenada, 1950–54', paper presented at the Conference on Political Sociology held at the University College of the West Indies, December 1961.

SMITH, T. E., 1962: 'Proposals for Malaysia', *The World Today*, vol. XVIII, no. 4, London.

SUBRAMANIAM, V., 1962: 'The Relationship between the Civil Servants and Ministers in India', *Journal of Commonwealth Political Studies*, vol. I, no. 3, Leicester.

SWAN, H. P., 1955: *Highlights of the Donegal Highlands*, Belfast.

TAEUBER, I. B., 1963: 'Demographic Instabilities in Island Ecosystems', in F. R. Fosberg (ed.), *Man's Place in the Island Ecosystem*, Honolulu.

TAYLOR, D. M., 1951: *The Black Carib of British Honduras*, New York.

THOMPSON, J. E., 1930: *Ethnology of the Mayas of Southern and Central British Honduras*, Chicago.

TITMUSS, R. M., and ABEL-SMITH, B., 1960: *Social Policies and Population Growth in Mauritius*, London.

TRINIDAD and TOBAGO, 1956: Central Statistical Office: *The Structure and Output of Industry: Report of a Census of Industrial Establishments 1953*, Port of Spain.

UNITED NATIONS, 1955: *Processes and Problems of Industrialization in Underdeveloped Countries*, New York.

WADDELL, D. A. G., 1961: *British Honduras: A Historical and Contemporary Survey*, London.

WARD, R. G., 1961: 'A note on Population Movements in the Cook Islands', *The Journal of the Polynesian Society*, vol. LXX, no. 1, Wellington, N.Z.

WARD, R. G., 1964: 'Cash Cropping and the Fijian Village', *Geographical Journal*, vol. CXXX, Part 4, London.

WELCH, C. E., 1962: 'The Senegambian Idea', *West Africa*, 22.12.62, London.

West Africa, 1965: 'The Gambia Goes it Alone: 1-4', 16.1.65, 23.1.65, 30.1.65, and 6.2.65, London.

WHYTE, W. F., 1943: *Street Corner Society*, Chicago.

WIGHT, M., 1952: *British Colonial Constitutions, 1947*, Oxford.

WILKINSON, R. C., 1949; *Report on the Project of Emigration from Mauritius to North Borneo*, Port Louis, Mauritius.

WILSON, G. and M., 1945: *The Analysis of Social Change*, Cambridge.

WRIGHT, A. C. S. and TWYFORD, I.: *The Soil Resources of Fiji*, Suva, in the press.

ZIMMERMAN, E. C., 1963, 'Nature of the Land Biota': in F. R. Fosberg (ed.), *Man's Place in the Island Ecosystem*, Honolulu.